Opioid Hell

THE SEEDY SIDE OF ADDICTION
TREATMENT-PHARMA-TRAFFICKING

Laura & Dylan Cole

ISBN: 979-8-987-2454-0-8 (Paperback)
ISBN: 979-8-987-2454-1-5 (Ebook)

West 4th St Publishing

To my son, Dylan, whom I deeply love and miss,
We Did It!
May this book find its way into the hands and hearts
of those in need of its message.

Author's Note

    I wrote this book to help families who may be struggling and alienated from the stigma of their child's addiction and mental illness. Or those like me, with years of battle scars, to be left only with a memorial of grief, love, and pain.

    Hopefully, I can reach parents before they leap into the uncharted, and at times fatal, world of addiction recovery centers and pharmaceutical pitfalls. My son was one of many who lost a battle to addiction, rehab corruption, pharmaceutical disasters, and fentanyl poisoning.

    To protect the innocent, I've changed all names of people and institutions.

Table of Contents

It never mattered to Dylan that he was science's pharmaceutical guinea pig; worse, his decision-making circuits were under-firing. My baby, son, and love produced a large payday for referral agents, rehabs, and sober homes.

Introduction

More than a dozen times, I witnessed my son Dylan's heroin withdrawal. The imagery of him kneeling on all fours, his knuckles bloody, still play out where his bed once stood. As do the echoes of him shrieking, trembling, sweating, and vomiting. I thought he'd die without medical attention the first time it happened. I called a drug addiction hotline and was quickly grounded by the volunteer. She told me what to expect and assured me it was unlikely he would die from heroin detox. Dylan would have flu-like symptoms for the next three days, and then the physical detox would end. It's called *dopesick,* and the window between that and euphoria was six to twelve hours. After experiencing each of his withdrawals, I couldn't imagine how anyone would want to relive such agony. But again and again, the demon reared its ugly head.

As he used and abused himself, I struggled to understand addiction, mental health, and whatever mistakes I may have made. We relied on medical professionals and addiction specialists during the early years — some were in it for money, some for science, and others, heart-centered. While Dylan swung between addiction and recovery, his brain struggled for *homeostasis*, the natural placement of chemicals in the brain that brings optimum results. When these chemicals go out of synch, so do we.

It never mattered to Dylan that he was science's pharmaceutical guinea pig; worse, his decision-making circuits were under-firing. My baby, son, and love produced a large payday for referral agents, rehabs, and sober homes. I begged him to stop using heroin and the doctor's prescribed meds, which would not cure his addiction. I was

After experiencing each of his withdrawals, I couldn't imagine how anyone would want to relive such AGONY. But again and again, the demon reared its ugly head.

All I had was

a decade's

worth of

experience

GRASPING

what I could

from books and

the internet to

save my son.

up against recovery centers, medical practitioners, and the world of big pharma. All I had to save my son, I grasped from books and the internet.

Every pharmacology cocktail, psych therapy, and addiction treatment threw us a curveball. For opiate addiction and detox, most medical practitioners prescribe psychotropics (psych) meds and Suboxone, an FDA-approved drug that combines two medicines, Buprenorphine and Naloxone. Buprenorphine is a synthetic opioid with a longer shelf life than heroin, meaning it lasts almost twice as long before withdrawal symptoms begin. It's combined with Naloxone, a non-addictive opiate blocker that prevents the addict from abusing opiates or the Suboxone.

The goal of Suboxone is to subdue the drug cravings, but if suddenly stopped it will cause detox and withdrawal symptoms like that of heroin.

The FDA put out a safety warning about dental problems reported by users of buprenorphine medicines such as Suboxone. Although people are losing their teeth, the article mentions that the benefits outweigh the risks. It's the doctor's responsibility to educate the patient. When starting Suboxone, attending an addiction-recovery program, (IOP) *Intensive Outpatient Program*, or (OP) *Outpatient Program* is suggested. You can read more online at FDA.gov.

I questioned how Dylan's brain would return to normal if most treatments consisted of brain-altering meds. What about his brain's natural ability to supply pain relief, mood stability, memory, sleep, energy, prevent depression, anxiety, and release of endorphins? I felt the meds would continue to enslave him in addiction and withdrawal and only slightly ease the mental desire for heroin. Would the rest of his life include psych meds, therapy, and meetings to silence heroin's siren calls?

After attending outpatient services, Dylan would return home annoyed, saying it was a waste of time and money. For hours he'd be forced to sit with other substance abusers, a situation that kept him grounded in his drug chasm. How could he embrace sobriety when his initial reasons for using drugs were still real and unaddressed?

So many of us conceal ourselves behind a secret curtain, slogging along with a pasted smile to survive another day of pointless chatter. How could I share that I was pulling a sweaty, detoxing child out of the bathtub an hour ago? Everything would be okay if I found his stash and got him through the three-day detox. No one would know I had lost sleep searching for heroin bundles (10 bags). My narrative was, *"I've got this!"*

No, that's not breakroom chat, not even close-friend chat. My inner hell reflected a saddened gaze and tilt of the head when I touched on the subject. No one wanted to face my ugly.

Entombed behind towel-covered windows, Dylan's nest reflected a solitary existence. There weren't days, nights, jobs, or people to see. His companion was his kit, a charred spoon, needle, tie, and ball of cotton for filtering the heroin. Painfully, I unraveled and plunged down the drug-infested abyss. It was as much a part of my world as it was his. The thread from which my heart dangled was thin. Horrors of addiction filled my waking hours with undue, wearying thoughts. My mind's eye had him burning to death while nodding with a cigarette. How can there be a hint of joy when life is so raw? When it began, I owned all of what happened; guilt, blame, it's a parent thing. What hadn't I done right?

When our children are young, we champion the battles while swinging our parental fists in the air. Again, our narrative is, *"I've got this!"* After a few more years of labor and love, we realize it was all an illusion. We're instantly humbled when the elementary school calls saying, "Come get your child; he's upset today." Suddenly, you're meeting with a school psychologist who squints through readers, asking, "How are things at home?" Life is no longer private, and your child is not the little, perfect one you began molding a few years back. When wearing my

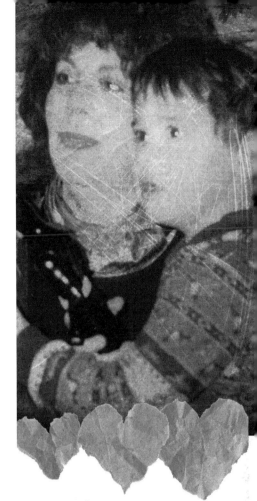

What hadn't I done right?

"Mom Cap," my feathers fluff like a peacock's, a fictitious power is bestowed on me, and I believed my drooling wee one would someday be everything I had wished: sensitive, life-passionate, and a seeker of truths.

I saw the same thing with peers, pacing with that new-parent vigilance in front of their den while marking their territory and keeping predators at bay. Unfortunately, calling the beginning of a child's life the "formative years" deludes us into believing that if we do our best, our child will develop into an emotionally sensitive, articulate human being, sharing our spiritual and humanitarian consciousness. They won't suffer from anxiety, depression, or insecurities. They won't be diagnosed bipolar or placed on meds to keep them socially acceptable. No, we've covered the bases.

When life suddenly became postponed and I was dethroned, my "Mom Cap" was traded for sunglasses that I hid behind for years. Many of us share the horror of losing a child to addiction. Or if, like me, you've lost one to an overdose, (*accidental overdose*) may this book help guide you to helpful resources. My opinions are from personal experience. I hope to enhance awareness and explain choices to those new to addiction recovery or still caught in its web.

With death comes the what-if's, should-haves, could-haves. At first, it's impossible to accept we are not responsible for our child's addiction and have no control over their destiny. Most of you reading this likely have experienced some of the available resources regarding addiction. If your child is still struggling, it's essential to do your homework and not rely entirely on medical experiments or addiction-recovery centers. My story is not unique but helps explain what can happen when we hand our loved one over to someone we believe will save, care for, cure, and return them whole again. The last thing we visualize is our child returning from rehab in a body bag.

Substance abusers are a BIG business, and frightened parents are even more profitable. We are vulnerable and quickly taken advantage of emotionally and financially. It's a broken system between substance abusers being trafficked for insurance fraud and exchanging their drug of choice for prescription meds.

Our loved ones can become victimized by medicine guesswork and recovery-center corruption. My son was one of them. He wasn't easy and verbally challenged authority figures. After his death, I was gutted and put a decade of journal entries away. Dylan wanted this book written and was part of it from the beginning. Two years after his passing, I picked up the pen again, and began to write.

The DSM-V-TR manual (Diagnostic and Statistical Manual of Mental Disorders) is produced by the American Psychiatric Association. The book contains diagnoses that Big Pharma can match with a new miracle pill. The DSM-5-TR book sales are in the multi-millions. Once my research began, I looked at the diagnoses and medicines prescribed during Dylan's emergency room, rehab, and psych-ward visits. There was a lot to learn about addiction, mental health, and what happens to the brain when it is chemically altered. I had believed an addictive substance solely caused addiction. I regret not focusing more on mental health, and never understood the brain's connection and potential for recovery. I was a parent, not a neuroscientist. It makes sense why substance abusers repeatedly relapse, and most current treatments are ineffective.

While writing this book, I refrained from including more chapters of our day-to-day personal struggles. The book's intent is to share a message that sheds light on a dark subject. I want to encourage those feeling helpless, that you are worth so much more than you imagine. Please don't detract from your child, or self, because of the stigma still tied to addiction and mental illness.

Ever since my son's passing in 2020, no longer ashamed, I speak openly about our struggle. So many people responded with their stories. Whether it was a parent, child, sibling or relative, each family suffered

Dylan wanted this book to be written and was part of it from the beginning.

I want to encourage parents to be proactive in their child's struggle with mental illness, addiction, and recognize that they are suffering terribly, and would rather not be living the way they are.

from addiction and loss. At times, I wondered had I not spoken first, would they have? Shame plays a huge part. If more people understood that addiction is not a question of willpower, we could make major strides. Thanks to social media, awareness of addiction, and mental illness is growing. The increased death rate from fentanyl poisoning, and unprotected borders are additional catalysts.

I want to encourage parents to be proactive in their child's struggle, and recognize that they are suffering terribly, and would rather not be living the way they are. If they're still breathing, there IS hope. Hope for you, as a loving parent who can seek answers. Hope for your child, that they will heal with proper medical treatment.

Take time to step away, breathe, and reflect on what is happening in your space. No moment is ever the same tomorrow. There's nothing more important for our well-being than love. I never found the source of Dylan's wound which entranced him to the world of heroin. I was occupied fighting his addiction, and often overlooked the person trapped behind the hideous mask. After his passing, I learned more about chemical imbalances, psych meds, and trauma.

As with many of your children, my son was an incredible person. His trademark was reaching out to everyone in need. We believed Dylan's future held a career in counseling, and he agreed. After his passing, there were many posts and private messages forwarded from those who felt had it not been for him, or how much he helped....

"Dylan helped me get back into my **LOVE** for art and really looked after me"

I was a human trafficking victim and I had and still do bad ptsd so they put me in a mental hospital after I was rescued I was really scared and Dylan helped me get back into my love for art and really looked after me in there and helped me get back into society once we both left we stayed in touch to keep each other in check and make sure we r both doing ok I sent a letter with my other pictures to let u guys know what a wonderful person he was and how he really changed me life I will forever be grateful for him and I would love is his son saw it one day to know how he really helped people and what a wonderful person he was

Of course! He has helped me in so many ways he would have been a fantastic councler he was the only person I talked to for months bc I just didn't feel ok talking to anyone else he helped me get back into society and now I'm back in college getting my degree In art I'm a junior now but I was able to do that because of him and because he never gave up on me no matter how cooko I got he will forever have a place in my heart and be apart of my healing bc without him coming into my life I would have probobly never made it out of the hospital

Dreams for Our Baby

Mother's

The baby's mother, my hopes, that organ will have a wonderful sense of humor and a creative spirit that just won't quit. I hope by the time he reaches puberty, that the world will be a safer, healthier, more opportune place to live in. I dream that step and I will instill in him all of the best from ourselves. I will teach him to value life and all of those who share in it. I will also teach him to fight for what he believes in - And not always look the other way as I have. He will feel this importance - and give back to the Earth. I dream that he will chase one career and master it. I dream that he will love and respect us as parents - and someday become a friend as well. I will encourage Eastern philosophys with an open respect to the West. I want to open his mind and heart to everything imaginable and then allow him his choice. I dream he will always find his inner balance. Yet always have the fight for survival. I dream that all of his dreams come ...

2-15-94
Date

1

Dreams for My Baby

Life is unpredictable, like roulette, and raising children falls into that realm. What catastrophic events might happen to my baby? Cancer, trafficking, sexual abuse, or something as horrific as murder? Some mothers never allow dark thoughts into consciousness, and other mothers' family jewels keep protected by deities, or the law of attraction, manifestos. My life's experience has canceled all prior beliefs and spirituality.

My baby journal held an array of hopes, wishes, and dreams. Dylan was an only child; he was adored and spoiled. We added opportunities for music, art, theater, and a heavy dose of computer gaming technology. Dylan's was the first generation introduced to Nintendo, PlayStation, and Xbox. When he was four, the computer held his interest with cheesy gun games, which he beat in no time.

When cradling our newborn, it doesn't matter if the diapers are lined with silk, cotton, or banana leaves. Nor does it matter if a child attended county college or NYU. Their chances are equal if addiction becomes their journey. Death leaves a calling card with each.

I was 37 when Dylan arrived, and back then considered a pregnancy risk, requiring an amniocentesis. However, it included the baby's sex, and when asked if I wanted to know, I happily replied, "yes." When asked what I wanted, I answered, "A boy."

Like most new mothers, I began making big plans, pasting affirmations, pictures, and words into my pregnancy journal. My childhood memories were mostly good, so my offspring would share a similar beginning.

My baby
journal held
an array of hopes,
wishes and
DREAMS.

By four,
I made an
appointment with
a child development
SPECIALIST.

Even though our family schedules didn't meet the criteria for sit-down dinners, Dylan would never eat alone at the table. With the boom of gaming and the internet, the absence of family time was real. Child rearing was a game of hide and seek, and lurking behind a bedroom door were the blue rays from TVs, computers, game systems, and cell phones.

Like a flint-carved arrowhead, my mothering skills were sharp. The internet was young, books still ruled, and I'd find the parenthood answer if needed. Around the time Dylan was 18 months, he began hitting his cheek on the floor. I read that this was a typical result of a baby's frustration, like head banging on the wall or crib. It's what babies could do, and the stage would pass. Dylan also woke from naps amid night terrors, and again, no need to worry; it was another childhood encounter.

Once Dylan could hurl his tiny legs over the crib frame, and up until his mid-school years, he came into my bedroom in the middle of the night to sleep. Early on, I spent a good deal of my sleeping hours returning him to his bed, only to hear his feet pitter-patter moments later.

Dylan's cheek hitting graduated to punching and would leave a bruise. Watching him hit his face was painful, and I tried many ways to intervene and make him stop. He often sported a bruise, and I had a videotape of him hitting his cheek to protect myself. Before he reached two, I brought him to a psychologist who had nothing to say other than, "How's the home front?" By four, I made an appointment with a child developmental specialist. After a couple of chat sessions, she asked me, "What are you afraid of?" I felt embarrassed as if I had the new-mother disease of overreacting when all I wanted were answers, tools, and solutions. I continued reading books as life moved forward.

Before pre-k, I enrolled Dylan part-time in a Montessori school whose philosophy I loved. Despite being shy and guarded, Dylan enjoyed the socialization and quickly made friends. My only struggle was getting him into the car after school. We had to be the last to leave, or I'd be hit and kicked when I picked him up. When he was born, I ruled that discipline would not entail hitting, which left me with many creative alternatives.

Upon reflection, I wouldn't say that Dylan was a cheerful child. His joy mostly present when we indulged him. Afterward, he was content with alone time and role-playing with his action figures. I encouraged a lot of creativity; by five, he had a drum set and weekly piano lessons, which he seemed to enjoy. He performed a Bach piece in second grade at his school's talent show. Dylan accompanied his grandmother to many musical productions at the local theater. He could sit quietly for two straight hours.

However, there was always something a bit off and different about Dylan. He wasn't like the other kids. He didn't want to learn how to ride a bike or join sports. I never pushed and allowed it to come to fruition when he was ready. His dad was a Tae Kwon Do black belt instructor, and Dylan agreed to give lessons a try. He quit when physical contact and sparing began. Still, there was no need for alarm. He had friends, was invited to birthday parties, and was received well by adults and teachers.

Why, then, did he often appear annoyed and unhappy? He'd never admit to having fun when we picked him up from a good-time event. Early on, he assumed a melancholy spirit. Our family vacations included several Disneyworld trips, and when a ride was over, he'd pout, be tired, and want to go home. Every dinner out turned into a battle, often ending with none of us talking. There was an invisible, underlying stress. My heart ached for answers while repeatedly trying to recreate happier scenarios. It seemed impossible to find Dylan's happy place. Even when we offered computer game design classes, he'd declined. His peers voiced their envy, wishing they had similar opportunities.

Dylan graduated from character costumes to collecting Pokémon cards. It was the rage, and I painted all of them on the basement walls. Absurdly, we agreed to pay a small

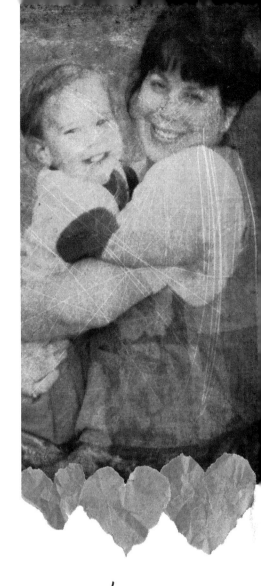

He wasn't like the OTHER KIDS.

Were these early signs of imbalance **BRAIN** lacking Seratonin or Dopamine?

fortune for some of the cards. It became an unquenchable thirst, like GameStop video games. We'd no sooner purchase a game for $65, then trade it for half the price the following week.

Was there something written on the wall that we missed, that was Dylan's segway to heroin addiction? Looking back on his childhood and what I know now, several unaccounted-for signs existed. If he had been hyper in class, a bully, and I, a more absent school mom, maybe the school would have suggested testing. Unlike teens, young children don't mask as well. But children do shift a lot in elementary school, and home situations can influence their day.

Dylan adored his third-grade teacher, and so did I. While attending a conference, the teacher made a small pinching gesture with his fingers saying, "Dylan has this much confidence." I was grateful for his honesty, but no matter how much cheering I did for Dylan, it wasn't absorbed. He had no problem telling me, "You're only saying that because you're my mom." Did he always feel insincerity from my words? Often it was a damned if I do, damned if I don't situation.

During his elementary years, I noticed Dylan's meltdowns increase. Most homework caused him to rub his face, breathe deeply, and peak with emotional overload. He'd toss things off the table and break pencils. I learned to walk barefoot on eggshells and remain one step ahead of him on good days. For the most part, my motherhood adventure isolated me. There were afterschool playground peers, but none discussed their child's imperfections. Those were well-kept, closet secrets. I continued researching during the early cyberspace days that didn't have dozens of web pages dedicated to a search word.

All I wanted for my child was for him to feel a sense of freedom and, within reason, say and do anything his heart desired.

When Dylan was born, and the nurse handed him to me, I unfastened his tightly wrapped blanket, opened his

arms, and welcomed him into the world. He would never be contained in a playpen, stroller, or hallway bouncy because I needed to cook and do chores. If his eyes were open, he would experience and explore, regardless of the aftermath's clean-up. His future held fearless ambitions. Those were my *mother's dreams* for my baby.

In the following chapters, you'll read that life fast-forwarded to a place where dreams don't come true. At least, not in the way I had envisioned. Each day brought a new threat, like that of a cresting river. In life's timeline, it happened quickly. Every parent knows the saying, "it felt like yesterday" when referring to their grown-up child. If the love I have for my son could have saved him, he would still be here. I work on embracing the three C's, and I couldn't (cause, control, cure) Dylan's substance abuse. A difficult lesson that I will battle for the rest of my life. The book's chapters don't follow the format of a chronological story. Instead, they contain compilations of journaled experiences, and what I learned from Dylan's text messages after his passing.

His

future held

FEARLESS

ambitions.

Had I only known the well-scripted, sales-motivated rep was half paying attention to a streaming video while waiting to capitalize on my innocence.

2

Band-Aids & Hope

I spent hours on rehab websites, the golden fleece of promises. The southwest would be a great place to recover; my son could gain sobriety while camping, horseback riding, meditating, attending IOP (intensive outpatient) meetings, and spa treatments. Today with sponsored paid ads, search online *heroin* or *drug addiction,* and immediately the sites appear. Each addiction-recovery site has a chat pop-up, and my guess is, many channel to the same hotline.

After discovering Dylan's heroin, I engaged with an 800 number, chat pop-up. She was welcoming, kind, authentic, and understanding of my plight. At the end of her sermon, I bit the bait. My heartstrings were taut, I was ashamed and vulnerable. I didn't care what it cost; I wanted my son to live the life I had wished. Had I only known the well-trained, sales-motivated rep, was one of many sitting in office cubicles, waiting to capitalize on my naivete.

After we established our text chat, she called directly, inquiring about insurance. Her computer keys clicked down a list of prospective facilities, following up with a price-plan offer of 30 to 90 days. If lucky, we might qualify for a scholarship! Each facility she mentioned had the best-trained staff, therapists, and medical professionals. Her script was well crafted for a parent's panic and desperation to save their child. They know we'd gladly remortgage a home, borrow from grandma, or cash out 401Ks.

When I began this chapter, I googled '*rehab scams.*' I was pleasantly surprised to find that word had spread. Unfortunately, when a parent discovers drugs on their child, they search for rehab, not rehab scams. They are oblivious

I was

ASHAMED

and vulnerable.

Her script was well crafted for a parent's panic and desperation.

Until

a gal pal

showed him

how to

punch his

FIRST

NEEDLE

into a

vein.

to the cycle of treatment, relapse, trading addiction drugs for psych meds, off-label options, and bipolar and manic-depressive disorder diagnoses. That's something that, if you are fortunate, you learn several rehab lessons later.

Many addiction-recovery facilities' practices are unethical and profit-based. In 2013, when my son entered his first rehab, it was when operating one didn't require special licenses. A recovering addict could open a facility with connections to an MD who'd write the prescriptions. It was easy to hang a sign outside, create a website, charge insurance companies a fortune with creative coding. Some states still haven't enforced regulations on these sorts of places.

The term "Florida Shuffle" describes how substance abusers are recruited for profit by referral agents. Addiction recovery centers pay the agents. A client already attending rehab can be offered money to relapse, reentering the detox phase of recovery for a minimum of seven to fourteen days. Insurance pays out more for detox. The referral agent scam is nationwide, and substance abusers are found in rehabs, AA/NA meetings, and on the streets. Once insurance benefits are verified, the referral agent connects with the recovery center who pays him the referral fee.

The sober house, where many stay between the IOP (Intensive Outpatient Program) and Alcoholics Anonymous, Narcotics Anonymous meetings, is usually supervised by a house manager (also in recovery). Unless printed clearly in the contract, they do not have medical staff in the facility's sober house. Doctors usually come to the IOP location.

By the time Dylan was 19, he had experienced several drugs, but heroin became his drug of choice. First, he snorted, then sold the heroin until a gal pal showed him how to punch his first needle into a vein. Years later, he said, "That's all it took, *one time.*"

My husband and I had purchased a retirement home in Arizona. A week before Dylan was going to drive out west with me, I discovered heroin in his room. I was slammed headfirst with the vision of a collapsed body, gritting teeth tightening a tie, and a finger flicking a needle before penetrating the vein. For me, heroin equated to death and the last call before the lights went out. My mother had passed six months before, and I buried my beloved aunt the day before the heroin discovery. Our moving truck was already en route and when Dylan agreed to attend rehab in Arizona, the pieces seemed to fit.

Finally, we could sleep. My son would gain sobriety in the addiction recovery's beautiful sober house. Although it's a decade later, only the fees have changed. Treatment provided extended care, evaluation, and periodic check-ups (depending on condition) by a medical doctor and addictionologist.

- Weekly one-on-one with a primary therapist.
- Rational emotive behavior therapy.
- Grief and trauma therapy.
- Family therapy sessions.
- Relapse prevention.
- Art/creation process.
- Spirituality group.
- Psychopharmacology group.
- Daily 12-step meetings.
- Daily house meetings.
- Weekly community meetings.
- Gym membership.
- Outdoor outings.
- The insurance rates for services:
  - PHP (Partial Hospitalization) $1,020.00.
  - IOP (Intensive Outpatient) $750.00 a day.
  - OP (Outpatient) $375.00 per day, three days a week.
  - Lab tests $1,300 per test, billed in addition to services.

The owner of this facility was a recovering addict with a voice that melted my tortured soul. She sent me this email:

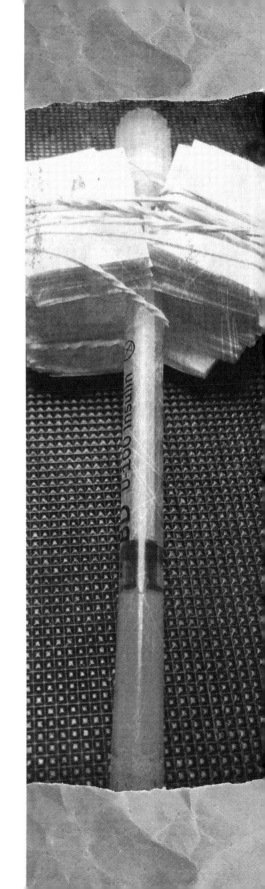

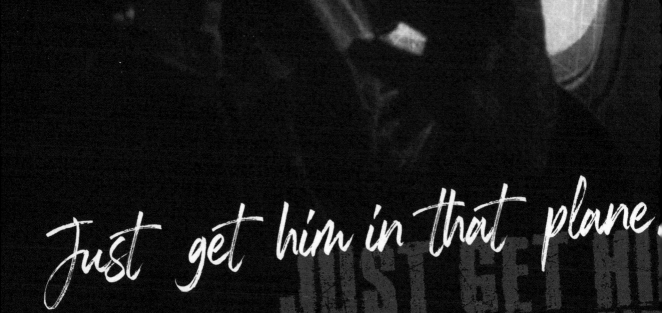

Finally, we could sleep.
  My son would gain sobriety in the addiction recovery's beautiful mansie

Just get him in that plane.

JUST GET HI
IN THAT PLANE

March 31, 1, 2013, at 4:16 pm

Hey Laura, just get him in that plane. It really does help us as a staff when the clients come in if they know the homeless shelter is next. Just know we will do everything in our power to give you your real son back. We will call you the minute we have him at the airport. You can call me Monday once he's on the plane with a credit card. If you need anything, don't hesitate to contact me.

While I was being fitted with blinders, early innocence smeared my heart. I didn't see Dylan's heroin use or the psych med experiments lasting a decade. Writing this chapter, hurts deeply because of the memory of a long, painful battle waged and what I had believed to be the truth. My email to the manager draws from my naivety:

April 1, 2013, at 4:05 am,

Dylan will soon board the plane. Is there anything you suggest for comfort while Dylan flies? He has jitteriness and aches. I read online about vitamin supplements etc., but that won't be immediate. I offered Advil, and he laughed. He couldn't sleep for the most part. I lay with him for a few hours while he said he was cold. Definite flu symptoms like I read. I don't know the severity of what he is feeling or going through. He's not asking for help per se. I was thinking more about the plane ride, his comfort, and any passenger sitting next to him? Is Xanax ok? My doctor won't give him anything, but I have Xanax from my aunt's collection. I'm not suggesting substituting one drug for another, only to get him on the plane to you.

She responded with "I can't suggest you do that, but if you do give that to him, it might take the edge off." As planned, when Dylan landed, he was met by the driver, who was also the house manager and a recovering addict. Wearing an iridescent wristband inscribed with the word *newbie*, my hand clutched an imaginary brochure of facts on detox and withdrawal complications. The rehab's owner

Early innocence SMEARED my heart.

I didn't ask
to see the
prescriptions,
and I didn't
understand the
detox protocol.
I had faith
in addiction
recovery programs,
medical staff, and
prescribed meds.
I never questioned.

promised Dylan would be medicated by a doctor as soon as he arrived. I innocently trusted the process.

Dylan's first week of rehab consisted of compacted bowels which caused him tremendous discomfort, and had he not passed them soon, he'd transfer to the emergency room. Had I thoroughly read the contract, I would have understood that a house doctor was on a "depending on the condition" as-needed basis. Constipation or diarrhea is a given during heroin and opiate detox.

I didn't ask to see the prescriptions or understand the detox protocol at that time. I had complete faith in addiction-recovery programs, medical staff, and prescribed meds. I never questioned.

We created a pharmacy account, so Dylan could receive various constipation treatments and other prescribed meds. I was grateful for the opportunity to talk with him; it was our first detox, and he was more than 2,400 miles away.

After about a week and a half, Dylan began his recovery program. I wish I had printed a picture from the website's beautiful sober house description. Our $14,500 a month bill included *Nutrition Education*, and looking back, I must laugh. That turned out to be the clients shuttled to a supermarket to purchase whatever they wanted, which would be waffles, sandwiches, and ice cream for Dylan. In addition, each week we were asked to transfer extra money on the card for incidentals and cigarettes.

By the second month, I began exchanging emails with Dylan's therapist. Some of his anger was dissipating, reflecting on past behavior. He gained privileges and rewards when participating in meetings and group activities. There was even talk of a community-service trip to South America. His therapist said he was very bright and knew how to get things *his* way. For the most part, it was a good report.

The rehab staff hosted a family weekend, and my husband flew to Arizona to attend. It had been several weeks since we last saw Dylan. That afternoon he looked happy, and all went well. We planned a couple of dinner dates for the following week.

At first, we weren't alarmed when Dylan said his housing had changed and he moved to a residential area. We were good if he was content with his roommates and house managers. When we pulled into the driveway, my gut's *uh-oh* clang detonated.

Dylan had relocated from the website's beautiful sober house with some other not-so-good boys into what I coined a frat house. They weren't necessarily 100 percent on board with the program. Dylan was not himself; he seemed overly sedated, and so did the other boys.

The house was filthy, with countertops covered with left-out food containers, and clothes hanging off furniture and piled on the floors. They all sat outside, chain-smoking while waiting for the next shuttle ride. After dinner, we dropped Dylan off back at the house. Doom and disappointment cast a shadow over the evening. I emailed Dylan's therapist:

June 23, 2013, 10:54 am
Hello Elaine,

I hope you had a good week, no need to answer this email asap. My husband went home, and I had quiet time. I'm processing last weekend with Dylan and two more visits with him. When you return to work, can you let me know if anything changed last week with Dylan's meds? He appeared fine during the family weekend, but during the week, on two occasions, we saw him around 3:30-4:00 pm, and he was out of it. He appears to be too sedated and zoned. He's almost lethargic. He's in there somewhere, but more out there. My husband felt the same way, so I thought I'd ask to see if any of the meds were changed during the week. It was disturbing to see the living conditions, but he says he wants to stay there and loves the house managers. I don't want to complain, but I feel like it's the last stop for the wayward. Or does the rehab put the long-term boys there and keep the lovely home for the newbies? I don't mean to put you in a position to explain, and I don't know who to talk to about this or whether I

should. Money-wise, it hurts. It's a fortune for us to keep him there. Between the house and Dylan's visible absence, it was difficult for us. I'm not feeling good about things.

The therapist responded:

June 26, 2013, 12:43 pm
Hi Laura,

I wanted to respond to both of your questions. The interaction I have with Dylan is like how you experienced it at the family weekend. He is engaged and doesn't seem too sedated. I will check with the psychiatrist today to see what's going on physiologically that could be causing Dylan to seem too sedated in the afternoon. Regarding his living situation, the house shouldn't be in that condition. They started shifting older residents to that house as we had more rooms in the last house that Dylan stayed. I must admit that the house that Dylan is at has some of our clients that are not doing so well. So that might be why they all look zoned out. I will still bring it up in staffing today as the clients should be here to get better, not as a holding tank where they can switch addictions.

DOOM

and

disappointment

cast a shadow over

the evening.

In another email, the therapist added that three other people had complained about the house's condition. I also learned that in addition to the other medicines, Dylan was prescribed sleeping pills. He told the psychiatrist he had difficulty sleeping, which was most likely true. Years later, I learned more about the effects of opiates on the brain; sleep issues were common during detox. As the brain rewires, it produces neurotransmitters with natural chemicals such as serotonin, creating melatonin, our sleeping aid. I wondered if sleeping pills would hamper the brain's ability to produce these natural chemicals, continuing the imbalance and inability to sleep naturally.

I followed up with the therapist, asking if the psychiatrist had changed the dosages of Dylan's meds. And what was up with his living conditions? Would this filthy,

rundown house cost the same per month, or would we receive a price break from the monthly $14,500, only made possible by a recent inheritance. I didn't gain much insight or get answers, as the therapist didn't want to jeopardize her position.

Like wild mustangs, struggling substance abusers were penned together to protect the newbies first admitted into the beautiful sober house, as depicted on the website's welcome page. How would that help the troubled boys, putting them in the same boat, and adding to their depression and sense of worthlessness?

Two weeks after the family weekend, my husband, in New Jersey, was in a catastrophic motorcycle accident. He was brought to a trauma center and underwent immediate surgery. He had more operations scheduled, but first, he had to be stabilized and induced into a coma. Before I could tell Dylan, his therapist took it upon herself. When I spoke with him, I held back the accident's severity because Dylan was experiencing grief, and in Dylan's style, it was coming out as anger. I kept in touch with the therapist, who wrote that Dylan was going to leave rehab and said he could do better independently.

I called Dylan; his monotonic voice raised the hair on my arm. Suddenly he had a distaste for the rehab and made his mind up to leave. When we hung up, I called his therapist, asking how medicated he was? She couldn't or wouldn't share the truth.

Dylan liked his house manager, who planned to open his sober house when he found a doctor to sign off on prescriptions. The therapist wrote me and said that Dylan was in a bad space regarding negativity and masking other emotions with anger. I was in the intensive care unit in NJ, bedside with my husband, begging Dylan to remain in the Arizona rehab. Less than a week later, with his father still listed as critical, Dylan left the rehab. At the time, the only saving grace was that he would remain in Arizona. It turned out to be a short-lived relief.

Struggling SUBSTANCE ABUSERS were penned together to protect the newbies.

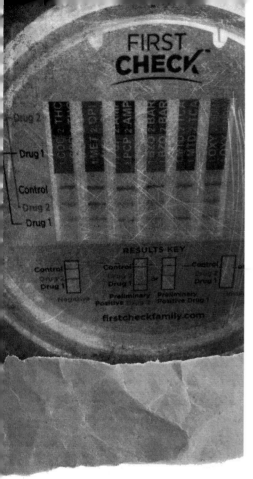

I was emotionally torn up And pulled between SQUATTERS and my husband.

Somewhere in the reserve of my soul, I held a glimmer of hope, placing my heart in trust mode. Should he return from rehab more mature and changed for the better, it will have been worth every tear shed and dime spent.

Dylan asked to cash in part of his grandmother's inheritance money to purchase a car. I agreed; he needed one to get to work. We kept in touch for a couple of weeks, I sent food money while he pursued work.

Once Dylan had wheels, he drove directly to the sober house. He became an outlaw to his first house manager, who was furious when three of his clients escaped with Dylan under cover of night.

While my husband underwent surgeries, the sober house manager tortured me with phone calls. He detested Dylan for tainting his supervisory image. The other kids' parents were upset, rightfully so. They, too, dropped a chunk of change on the rehab promise. Worst of all, where were their kids? Dylan's therapist sent an email that word on the street was that Dylan and the three other kids had relapsed and were using my new home in Arizona as a base.

Pumped with angst, I envisioned them squatting in my dream home that I had spent years planning for and only lived in eight weeks myself. The saying "You take yourself wherever you go" couldn't be truer. I ran but could not hide. My joy was fleeting as the all too familiar, dark shadow had returned.

How do I do this? I was emotionally torn up and pulled between squatters, and my husband, who had been reawakening from an induced coma. He was unable to walk, talk, or think. After gathering enough support from friends and co-workers to look after him, I headed back to Arizona to face the nightmare.

I experienced my first lesson about a substance abuser's ability for detachment. How could my son not care that his father, in intensive care, was fighting for his life? Or me, for that matter, who was under tremendous stress? If I were he, I'd be sitting bedside with my father while reassuring my mother.

At this time, a war divided a mother's love for her child against the uncontrollable demonic forces of his addiction. A beautiful soldier was about to step on a landmine, and a mother's love was knee-deep in the trenches. At the time, I was completely clueless of how to help Dylan. How to sustain my arsenal to combat an army far greater than mine?

When my plane landed in Phoenix, I called and startled Dylan saying, "I'll see you soon." The scene following my call was easy to imagine, and my gut, the informer, told me it wouldn't be good. It would be the first of many such scenarios.

As I expected, each of the escaped kids ran for it, leaving behind their possessions in the house. In the wake of everything, the house looked like a crack den. Each room had its share of dirty dishes and toilets jammed and covered in vomit. My ferret's cage was tucked into a dark bedroom, caked with fecal matter a couple of inches deep. My new friend had met me at the house, and we began the arduous task of bagging the garbage.

My ransacked new home was emotionally violating and, I didn't know where Dylan and the others were. Days had passed without a word. Eventually, the kids ran out of their parent's generosity and headed to the airport to return home. Their parents, including myself, had thrown away well over $50,000 for the rehab's golden fleece of promises.

After a few days, Dylan, still in Arizona, grew tired of sleeping in his car and called, begging to come back. He asked if I'd allow a girl from the rehab to stay. Of course, I said yes; hope was still controlling my heart. They were ready to work on a new life, and agreed to remain sober, and attend therapy and meetings.

I was now a graduate of Heroin 101 and began to tune into the signs when Dylan was using. His hygiene was abysmal, his hair greasy enough to look freshly showered. He was often asleep in a darkened room with no appetite,

A war divided a mother's love for her child against the uncontrollable demonic forces of his addiction.

and if eating, it would be something sweet like chocolate milk, waffles loaded with syrup or ice cream.

Dylan's psych meds from rehab were running out. We were in a small town in northern Arizona, with a sparse number of medical professionals; we couldn't find a doctor whose waitlist was less than three months, and most psychiatrists were no longer accepting new patients. I didn't have experience then, only a gut trying like hell to guide me. I wrote to Dylan's sober house therapist, asking for the psychiatrist's name who had prescribed his meds. Dylan needed a refill of Seroquel and Escitalopram.

A few years later, seasoned with dozens of psych med scripts, Seroquel appeared to top the list for treating bipolar, depression, and schizophrenia. I felt it was nothing more than a patch. Dosages are flexible and monitored by the doctor and patient. Escitalopram is used to treat depression and anxiety. It helps restore the balance of certain natural substances (serotonin) in the brain. The early days of Dylan's addiction and rehab could not meddle with heroin's blanketing love and serenity.

Now a

graduate of

HEROIN

101.

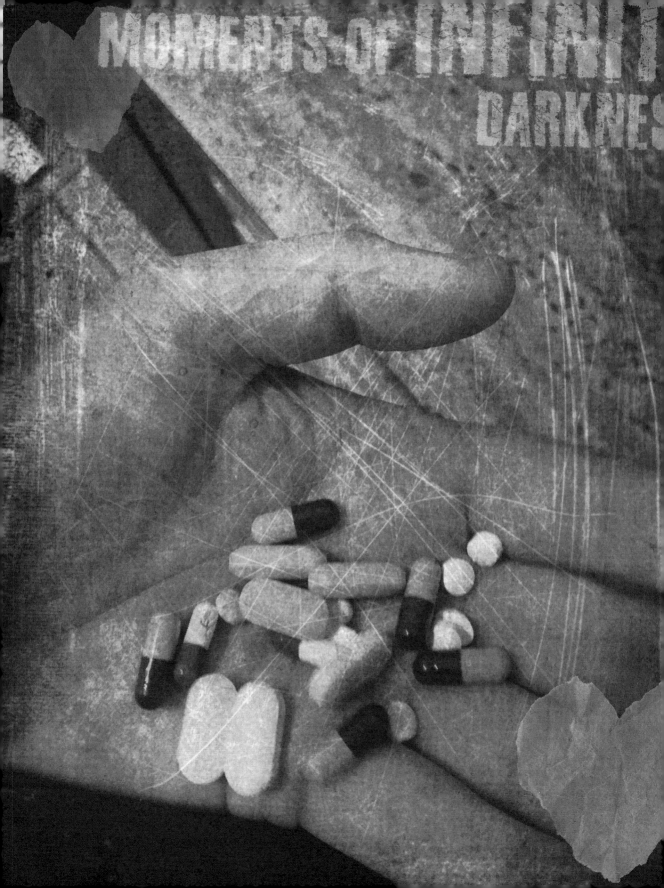

MOMENTS OF INFINITY
DARKNESS

Acceptance

We are not handed a tabbed binder with directions and coping skills for parenting a child with drug addiction. My mom powers faded when my son reached 18, but they were an illusion in the first place. Should Dylan have been kicked out of the house during the early days of drug use? Is this where most of us go wrong and assume the title of enabler? Rehabs are bandages of hope, and they fall off. Don't be tricked by fancy websites, pictures, and horseback rides. Read the contract's fine print and know that unless written otherwise, there are NO REFUNDS for early discharge.

I was petrified of losing Dylan to the streets, crime, prison, and death. As parents, we offer a comfortable home, food, unconditional love, and hand over control. It didn't matter that my son's thorned body armor found my triggers and bled me unconscious. I existed with shallow breath and a fledgling heartbeat, sustained by moments of infinite, emotional darkness.

I'm not sure what my biggest fear was. My pride was a huge factor in concealing the truth, and hiding it was a challenging daily chore. I had a business that involved teaching 100 students a week. I had to be happy, engaged and remember everyone's story. I entertained birthday parties, Girl Scout and Boy Scout troops, after-school enrichment, and assisted senior housing programs. I maintained a creative atmosphere while rotting in aching sadness inside.

By the time Dylan reached 19, the little boy I once coddled replaced my hug with a squeeze of a belt and my kiss goodnight with a syringe prick. No matter how long I

REHABS

are band-aids

of hope,

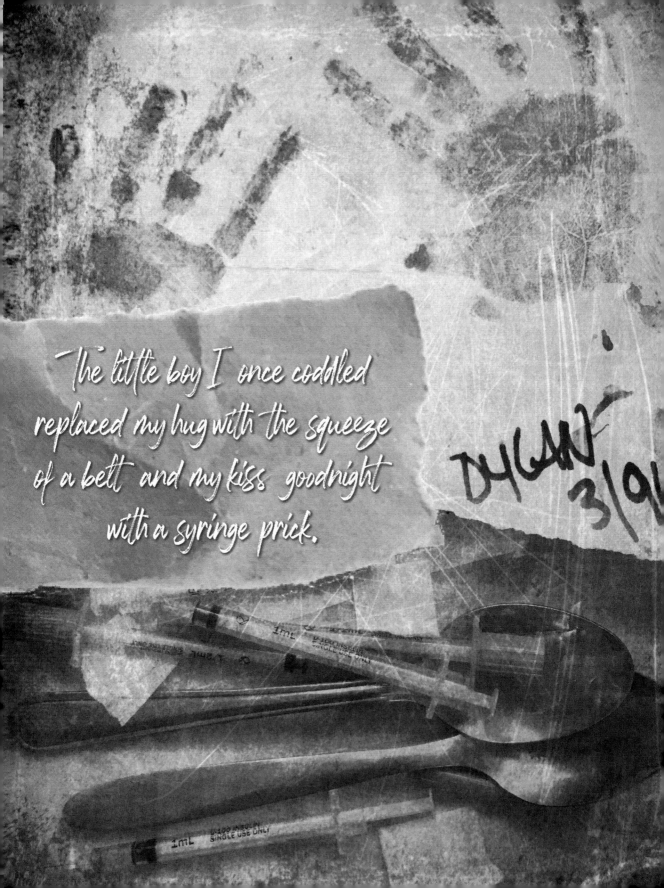

The little boy I once coddled replaced my hug with the squeeze of a belt and my kiss goodnight with a syringe prick.

DYLAN 3/9

stared at him, searching deeply into his eyes, I didn't know him. I was frightened by him and for him. He had no fear of authority figures, including the police. It was like he was a character from someone else's novel. I kept asking myself, "Who is this?" "Where is my son?" I was afraid of this person and locked my bedroom door at night. We start with the baby's first-word journal, dozens of pictures, videos, and each tooth tucked into the fairy box. I saved every drawing, action figure, and Pokémon card, packing them away for a much-expected bright future.

I believed that youth was on Dylan's side, the world awaited him, and this too, shall pass. Famous people have shared our story and moved on to incredible success in life. My son was an astonishing candidate for so much more. He was tall, handsome, and everyone adored his charisma. He had a fantastic, witty, and dark, sense of humor. I kept looking into the future, seeing what I wished the outcome to be. Again, this was going to pass.

I discovered he was dealing drugs when he was in eleventh grade. We installed an alarm system on windows and doors when the battles began. We decided who was allowed into the house, and we had our share of kicking some out. I knew many teens experimented — my husband and I did at his age — but not many graduated to a "Scarface" status.

Once a senior in high school, he found gratification in dealing cocaine and marijuana. His earnings far exceeded his friends' legit paychecks. He was finally on top for someone who suffered from insecurity and depression. I became a detective patting down every inch of his bedroom. The evidence was always there, including my beloved poetry book with hollowed-out pages hiding a wad of cash.

Dylan's father and I tried convincing him how well he could do in business, sales, and marketing. He was great at researching subjects of interest, especially law. If only he would switch his energies from negative to positive. Three months before graduating high school, he

The

WORLD

awaited him, and

this too shall pass.

There would not be prom or graduation photos over our mantel. The future had TERROR, *not excitement, and my beautiful boy was going strong into the dark side.*

dropped out. He was 19, and the school suspected him of drug dealing. Every time I believed the pain couldn't get worse, it did.

My peers were visiting colleges, sharing the excitement and joy of their child's future. Politely, I'd listen while holding my breath to prevent tears. There would not be prom or graduation photos over our mantel. The future held terror, not excitement, and my beautiful boy was heading directly into the dark side.

What happened to the last 12 years of costumes, artwork, achievements, and holiday cards with tissue flowers? What did I do wrong? My husband and I became significant enablers, purchasing musical equipment, computers, Xbox, iPad, and anything else, hoping he'd switch sides. We thought encouraging his strengths would work and change the dark to light. He was on the cliff's edge, and we provided the parachute. What appeared to be a teenage phase would end someday, and everything would be all right. He was terrific in so many ways.

The train lost its brakes and veered off the track, but we caught him in our net. Year after year, we never ran out of our hope rope. We supplied him with cell phones, cigarettes, and at times, even alcohol when he threatened, he'd return to heroin. In my heart, my son was never to be a statistic, and it was something we discussed often as his buried friend list grew. It took me years to accept that I may never have a happy home or life-ending.

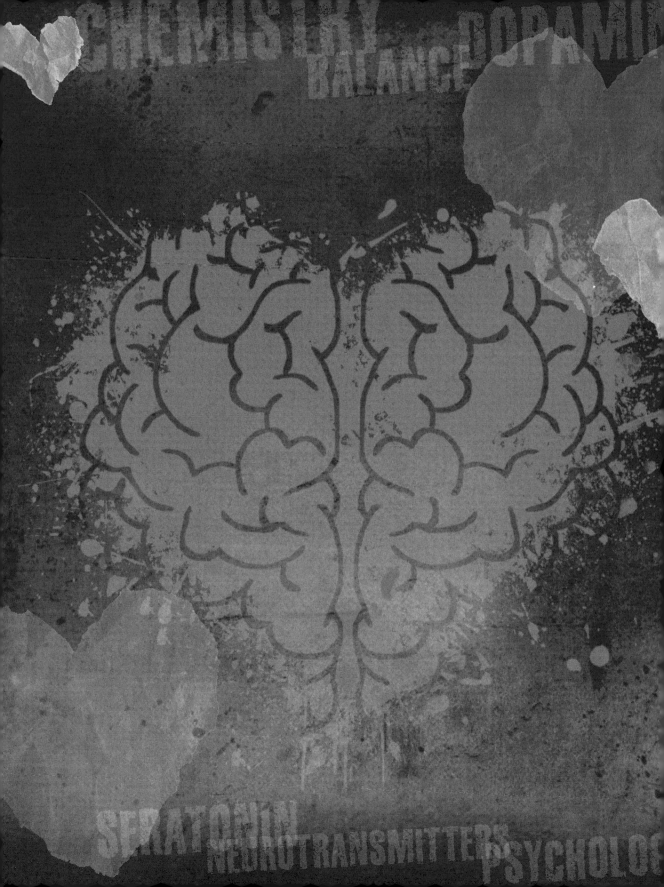

4

The Addicted Brain

Our journey took its share of twists and turns, and I continued asking myself what science, medicine, and addiction recovery offered my son. And in the end, would my ideas have kept him alive? My intuition and doubts led me to read dozens of medical articles about addiction and brain chemistry. Initially, it was intimidating, sifting through government sites of the National Library of Medicine (NLM), the National Institute of Health (NIH), nlm-nih.gov and the National Institute on Drug Abuse (nida) nida.nih.gov.

Doctors' lab, tests, theories, and psychology had spanned years. I began to understand some of the medical terminologies, and the balance of our neurotransmitters such as dopamine's *feel-good/reward,* serotonin's *sleep/appetite*, GABA *'relax calm,'* and acetylcholine's *'muscles memory.'*

There were so many studies on each of these neurotransmitters that produce chemicals necessary for our bodies to function. If you add drugs or alcohol to the body, the neurotransmitters become imbalanced. In most cases, they'll return to their natural balance if you remove the drugs and alcohol from the body. There are several factors that will determine the brain's rewiring time.

By gaining insight into the personal struggles of Dylan's brain chemistry, and the consequences to his mental health, my heart began to reopen. I wondered; if he were still alive and I shared this knowledge, would he have been receptive? Not one medical professional, or addiction specialist, ever suggested this concept. All we experienced was a bombardment of psych meds and Suboxone. Quick

By gaining insight into the personal struggles of Dylan's brain chemistry, and the consequences on his mental health, my HEART began to reopen.

Doctors never suggested tests to determine these IMBALANCES.

fixes, money-makers, and lack of time and education contribute to inadequate options for addiction recovery. There was a reason why Dylan needed to be numb. Psych meds would continue to repress an unspoken, possible trauma.

I had confirmation that I wasn't far off with my fixation on Dylan's meds. I had wanted him to stop them after the physical detox ended. I'll never know how much the meds had to do with playing pinball in his brain and why exercise and nutrition were underemphasized. The meds were a synthetic version of something our brains create, and if there's an imbalance, what alternatives are there?

For Dylan, the meds perpetuated his brain's inability to find equilibrium. Unless closely monitored by a medical doctor specializing in neuroscience and addiction, the meds can be dangerous; and, in Dylan's case, useless. It's also futile and detrimental to prescribe meds when there's a risk of them being combined with other substances. Substance abusers may neglect to take them correctly, adding to their mental instability. The meds don't cure, and at best, they bring relief to withdrawal symptoms. I understood why doctors pulled out their blue pads; their job was to assist the patient, reduce withdrawal symptoms, and help prevent relapse. It's all they had to offer.

When I read the studies of dopamine imbalance, it looked like a roadmap of Dylan's life. It controls the brain's pleasure and reward center. Running, dancing, shopping, chocolate, music, drugs, and alcohol, all produce dopamine. I questioned how long his levels could have been misfiring. Was Dylan's addiction due to a feeling of inadequacy, which inevitably brought him into the dark world of self-medicating? He wanted the light off and the pain to be gone.

Doctors never suggested the tests that could have possibly determined chemical imbalances. Neurotransmitters such as Serotonin and GABA, if imbalanced, have a lot to do with the psyche, depression, anxiety, sleep, calming, and feeling good. Dylan struggled with all of them. I never understood which deterioration came first: drug-induced or mental health. The only meds Dylan received were for bipolar and major/manic depression diagnoses, and psych medicines that don't cure addiction. When all else failed, a diagnosis of bipolar was fitting and enough for an insurance payout.

Everyday addiction to drugs or alcohol spikes dopamine in the brain, which reduces its daily production. When substance abusers stop using, the brain starts the process of rewiring. Hormones that control the output of pleasure, memory, mood, sleep, pain, etc., are not being produced at the average rate, causing downward mood swings, lack of motivation, concentration, and more — all this information filled in the puzzle. For years, Dylan's brain never had a rest. If he wasn't using heroin, he took other narcotics, prescribed meds, or alcohol. If he wasn't dangerously mixing them together, he was neglecting to take his meds as prescribed.

The National Institute on Drug Abuse and the American Psychiatric Association describes addiction as a mental illness. The DSM-5-TR *Diagnostic Statistic Manual* lists it as SUD *Substance Use Disorder,* which is labeled a *mental health illness*. Not all professionals in the field of science and addiction agree on this subject.

I delved deeper into books and online resource material on addiction, supplements, ending cravings, and pharmacogenetic testing, which aids in medicinal decision-making. It's fascinating, but there's often a jury out deliberating. Everything I read seemed to make sense; having a diagnosis such as SUD can be covered by some insurance. Clinical testing, studies, and mental health awareness educate the public that much of this is out of the substance abuser's hands.

In addition, I came upon Orthomolecular medicine, which focuses on the whole body, its deficiencies, and its imbalances. Again, the word biochemistry appeared. From

Dylan's brain NEVER had a rest.

There are times when it feels endless, HOPELESS, and even fateful.

there, I found Dr. David Gersten's website which included integrative psych and nutritional medicine. The amino-acid therapy charts and information is incredible. If you want further information, search aminoacidpower.com. Several websites offer Integrative Medicine's whole-body approach with nutrition, and biochemistry testing. At the very most, it's the healthiest way to find answers and methods to best help someone suffering from mental illness and substance abuse. These are not medically unorthodox methods but joined forces. Don't forget trauma and addiction, which can be the root cause for someone wanting to turn off, shut down, and escape.

I recommend keeping a journal of your website searches. Until writing this book, I did not know of PAWS (*post-acute withdrawal syndrome),* protracted withdrawal syndrome, or prolonged withdrawal syndrome. Be careful if you use the word PAWS in a search, nine out of ten times; you'll be brought to a rehab's page with an 800 number. It's best to go directly to samhsa.gov (substance abuse and mental health services administration) or NIH (nida.nih.gov).

Much of what I learned confirmed Dylan's behavior during a sober spell. He continued to be tired, cranky, anxious, easily agitated, and depressed. The symptoms could last months to a couple of years. Of course, the duration of PAWS is based on the substance used, how much, and often, it was used. The substance abuser must learn to manage sleep, nutrition, triggers, therapy, mindfulness, meditation, and more. It's essential to have a support system.

I spent many detoxes with Dylan and supplied healthy alternatives, and no, he was not receptive. Not enough time elapsed between sobriety and using. Neither of us understood what was happening within his brain. Undoubtedly, his brain circuits were not firing correctly, affecting his choices and decision-making. His use of heroin had spiked his dopamine levels to the point where his brain was altered. It was an incredibly painful and

vicious cycle to live. It would take more time to heal than Dylan was willing to tolerate.

Taking a deeper dive into the psych end of addiction is the world of trauma. Many books refer to childhood trauma being the culprit for addiction. Books written by the Dr. Gabor Mate, 'In the Realm of Hungry Ghosts,' and 'The Myth of Normal,' are excellent. Dr. Gabor can easily be found online as a guest speaker through many social media webinars and podcasts. The Body Keeps the Score, written by Dr. Bessel van der Kolk, is another must-read.

There are times when it feels endless, hopeless, and even fateful in the throes of our child's addiction. Our souls are yanked forcibly through the gates of misery. When I began writing this book, I didn't realize it would touch on brain chemistry. There's much more I wanted to write about in this chapter, but I am not qualified to do so. I'm grateful to have been provided with some answers about my son's struggle. I found what made sense in a place where karma, medicine, religion, and spirituality had failed.

There are options, and it's up to you to do your homework. Find an integrative doctor who will perform a series of tests or an addictionologist who has studied neuroscience and addiction. Although one focuses more on brain chemistry, it's at least a start in the right direction. The book *Brain in Balance, Understanding the Genetics and Neurochemistry Behind Addiction and Sobriety,* written by Fred Von Stieff, M.D., is written in a manner everyone can understand. Everyone in addiction, recovery, therapy, and medicine should read it, as well as students and substance abusers.

How much inner turmoil was Dylan suffering, and how hard it must have been for him? He felt different and created a unique persona to carry him through. Throughout school his teachers liked him and didn't understand why he did poorly. Even before drugs were involved, the school made no suggestions for IEP (*Individualized Education*

Which

SYSTEM

failed him?

Program) testing. Which system failed him, or was it a mixture of everything? His brightness was heavily shadowed by the unknown.

When Dylan was in high school, my husband and I decided to have him neurologically tested at a local children's hospital. It included tapping on the knee, memorizing paragraphs, numbers, and in the end, a complete waste of time. Was the belief that Dylan was scamming to get out of schoolwork? Had there been something wrong, how did he get as far as eleventh grade? We were still desperate for help and made an appointment with a psychiatrist who specialized with teens.

Dylan's school performance fit into the common ADD (attention deficit disorder) diagnosis. The psych doctor performed the usual tests and came up empty-handed. He felt Dylan might have a touch of ODD (Oppositional defiant disorder). I love that one; what teen doesn't have ODD? However, at Dylan's request, the doctor agreed to prescribe Adderall, which may keep him focused and alert in school. The Adderall didn't last a month. Dylan said it upset his stomach too much. Later we'd learn he wanted it for the sole purpose of getting high — and trading it for other drugs.

An active overdose has the choking, gurgling, and snoring death sounds; it is the death rattle.

5
Help Is on The Way

If you're reading this book, you've already shared a few dreaded lessons, and maybe you've also fallen to your knees while hovering over an unconscious child gasping for air. Unless you've lived a similar moment, it's unimaginable and hard to describe.

I dialed 911, stayed on long enough to give my address, then tossed the phone onto the bed. We were in rural NJ, which made waiting for the EMT an eternity. Between blowing air into my son's mouth and hearing his lungs expand, I shouted, "Where the fuck are the EMTs?" I continued to push on his chest, screaming, "Dylan, is this how it's going to end?" An active overdose has choking, gurgling, and snoring death sounds; it is the death rattle.

When the EMTs finally arrived, my heartbeat was pulsating through my neck. The cranky medic who had become familiar with our house sauntered to the basement with attitude. He told me we needed to get Dylan onto the floor so he could inject the Narcan. Not an easy task with the dead weight of a six-foot-three, two-hundred-pound body. As soon as we had Dylan on the mattress' edge, his eyes slit open.

Abruptly the medic dropped his grip on Dylan's legs like hands coated in grease. He leaned into his shoulder's walkie-talkie, snapping, "cancel the call," then mumbled to me, "He opened his eyes, so he's not overdosing, but we're taking him to the ER."

After that traumatic experience, I shifted to the usual business, stood on the pedestal, bowed my head,

I SCREAMED

"Dylan, is this how it will end?"

and received my ribbon for a mummified existence. There wasn't time to collapse crying in a bed, my jovial, three-year-old grandson, wanted to play with dinosaurs. These moments reveal our invincibility.

The year 2018 introduced a myriad of overdoses. My detective skills were no match for Dylan's addictive ones. Often the signs were overshadowed by my motherly hope. The blanketed hug of heroin creates a calm, like a twilight snowfall, and Dylan's door was beginning to close. I put on my gloves and dusted for prints. It wasn't long before I found heroin, needles, and empty vials that had likely held crack cocaine.

His story was an artwork of trilogies, and crescendos, and this was the last act. The scatter of dealer-stamped glassines (containers for heroin) looked like candy wrappers — each representing a romantic interlude with the syringe's punch. Nod burns pierced holes in the bedsheets from Dylan falling asleep with lit cigarettes.

If I had dropped my son onto an abandoned island, would he have remained a heroin addict described as major depressive or bipolar? Teen obituaries join the ill and elderly. It's horrific, and we think we can control and fix everything. Often, I held my breath while opening Dylan's bedroom door, fearing vapored air and his graven blue face.

When I brought Dylan home from the ER, we discussed trying a methadone clinic, a treatment that's been around for decades. A medical professional dispenses methadone in an addiction clinic and monitors the medicine levels in the blood and urine. There weren't clinics in our rural area, but Dylan found one with early-morning appointments in an adjoining county. It was a challenge due to time, distance, and rush-hour traffic. I developed more concerns when he shared that some substance abusers continued to use while taking methadone.

The clinic ran a tight ship with a firm and strict schedule. Within a month, Dylan missed two appointments, the second a holiday. New Year's Eve

His story was an artwork of trilogies, crescendos, and the LAST ACT.

weekend meant he'd miss receiving the extra doses he needed to sustain him until the clinic reopened. We spent the holiday detoxing in the ER. It was as ugly, painful, and equal to heroin withdrawal. He never returned to the methadone clinic.

Another month passed when Dylan began discussing Ibogaine (a natural psychoactive plant found in the African rainforest) treatment and its value in detoxing. He had spoken with a young recruiter of an Ibogaine clinic in Mexico. Together we watched YouTube videos promoting Ibogaine with the clinic, owner, and client testimonials. After a few conference calls with the recruiter, who would shadow Dylan and be our liaison, we paid $15,000 and booked his flight.

The United States does not authorize Ibogaine treatment, however, it's accepted and practiced in Canada and Mexico. Ibogaine does offer immediate relief from withdrawal symptoms and cravings. That's a huge benefit for substance abusers, who in the U.S. continue to be addicted, and suffer withdrawal symptoms from doctor prescribed, pharmaceuticals.

Going back several decades in the U.S., science and the government have done their share of LSD experiments, some successful. It ended during the Nixon administration and the creation of the Controlled Substance Act. LSD was labeled a 'Schedule 1 Substance,' making it illegal to prescribe or possess.

LSD has been reintroduced to some psychiatric departments, and is practiced in clinical trial settings, until the FDA gives the green light. Read online about *Psychedelic Assisted Therapy* for treating mental disorders, PTSD, addiction, trauma, anxiety, and depression with psilocybin, MDMA, and ayahuasca. But be aware there are opportunists online who for a fee, will babysit you while you trip out. They do not supply the psychedelic, that you'll have to acquire yourself. Dylan was a believer in Ibogaine, which is what brought him to Mexico for detoxing.

I brought Dylan home from the ER, and we discussed a methadone clinic.

MEXICO

The United States does not authorize Ibogaine treatment.

It was difficult enduring Dylan being in a foreign country, participating in an experiment to reverse the ill effects of withdrawal by inducing hallucinogenic ones. He couldn't wait to experience what he called *breaking through* to the other side. His thirst for the unknown and beyond was limitless.

The duration of the medically supervised Ibogaine treatment was about ten days. After Dylan's first session, he videotaped himself super chilled sitting poolside. He said with the Joker's smile, "I'm never coming home, I'm staying here forever."

The only thing that ever-dulled Dylan's blade had been heroin. There had never been a pause in life's madness, and we weren't sure how to react. Was this heroin detox, with no screaming, vomiting, or punching walls? Was this a time of rejoicing, our Phoenix Rising?

A few days passed when a clinic employee suffered an overdose of street drugs but survived. The clinic's owner became enraged, yelling at the unconscious victim. According to Dylan, he said, "Leave him there to die." The incident seriously triggered Dylan, disillusioned with disrespect for the clinic's owner, yet he asked if we'd pay to extend his treatment. We agreed to pay for another ten days. His quest for the ultimate breakthrough kept his focus and for us, provided hope. In our life, no stone has been left unturned.

Dylan tossed us the chum of photos that included meditations, beach walks, drum circles, and smudging ceremonies. Here's one of his recorded hallucinogenic Ibogaine experiences:

My first trip, I didn't see much. But I saw a ladder with steps falling, and I grabbed the last one. My second trip, I dealt with the violent image of shooting an old friend's entire family. I saw the love of my life in a three-way. I saw five gravestones. And many dead bodies. My last trip was emotional. I saw my funeral with wooden doors opening and people walking it, and it hovered over my casket. I saw my mom as an old

His quest for the ultimate breakthrough kept his focus and, for us, provided HOPE.

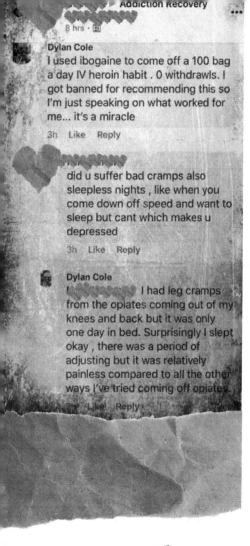

8 hrs ·

Dylan Cole
I used ibogaine to come off a 100 bag
a day IV heroin habit . 0 withdrawls. I
got banned for recommending this so
I'm just speaking on what worked for
me... it's a miracle

3h   Like   Reply

did u suffer bad cramps also
sleepless nights , like when you
come down off speed and want to
sleep but cant which makes u
depressed

3h   Like   Reply

Dylan Cole
I had leg cramps
from the opiates coming out of my
knees and back but it was only
one day in bed. Surprisingly I slept
okay , there was a period of
adjusting but it was relatively
painless compared to all the other
ways I've tried coming off opiates.

Like   Reply

I saw my

FUNERAL

with wooden doors

opening and people

walking in.

nanny. I saw my dad passing from old age, which made me cry. I saw myself shooting up. Overdosing. I saw myself sober I saw Jackie and me finally happy. I saw Damian grow up. I saw what my life could and will be, and I will fight for the life my loved ones and I deserve. It has been amazing, and I feel like a new man, Dylan; I know you will struggle with dealing with life, but please be strong. You promised that if you ever stick a needle in yourself, you will kill yourself. Always remember... estoy renacido

Dylan asked for souvenir money. He was anxious to bring something back for each of us, especially for his son. It wouldn't be the first time that he instead gifted himself. This time with a slick-backed haircut, cigars, and tattoos. One over his eyebrow, with the words '*estoy renacido*' (I am reborn), and the other, a broken needle right below the eye. I was crushed, not about him lying about souvenirs, but for the facial tattoos; he was so young and handsome. What about the rest of his life and his son?

He apologized, saying the tattoos were necessary, a constant reminder of his sobriety. It felt again as if we were being betrayed, lied to, and this was nothing more than a vacation. While in treatment, he relapsed with alcohol over a phone fight with his girlfriend. We didn't know what to expect when he returned. It was disheartening that nothing seemed to work, but disappointment never stopped us from hoping. I revamped his living space with new furniture and accessories. I wanted Dylan to feel a fresh new start.

When he returned home, he wasted no time pursuing where to purchase Ibogaine and found a source in Canada. He hooked up with his friend, took LSD, and spent a good deal of time sleeping. It seemed like the same old Dylan.

It didn't take long, about a month, when Dylan's former self emerged. The angry, short-fused, drug-induced one. His heroin habit increased tenfold, and he no longer hid the evidence. The cocktail mix of powder, pills, rocks, and booze bonded to the new tabletops. Empty glassines filled soda cans and ice cream containers. I imagine his mirror reflecting the broken needle, reborn tattoo, would bring deep self-loathing and quickly return him to heroin's infamous warm hug.

The new digs returned to their sinister past, with darkness, ashes, and debris. Dylan's battle losses were ours, too; we each felt defeated. It seemed like the Ibogaine experience was another sandbox. It's just not that simple. Whatever pill, program, or therapy employed, there was much aftercare work to be done — the part which made Dylan's potential for sobriety next to impossible. Why someone is looking to shut down cannot be ignored.

Ibogaine is not a cure for addiction, but it does provide a more comfortable detox. No addiction-recovery center offers a cure. Much more work awaits the substance abuser's desire and discipline for sobriety. The Ibogaine clinic owner stressed the same to Dylan. All I'm saying is, please do not be misled by a poster child, believing any one thing will be the magic bullet. The following is a social media post of Dylan's that holds a lot of ground supporting Ibogaine.

Oct 26, 2019

Ibogaine is a miracle substance. Anyone who tries to argue different is ignorant to the truth.

The only reason it is illegal in the U.S. is because Big Pharma is making way too much off creating addicts. You're in pain? Here's an Oxy, you're hooked on Oxy? Here, try Suboxone and rehab.

Still struggling? Spend fifteen grand on an inpatient and perhaps try Methadone or Subutex in place of Suboxone. All these alternatives are just switching crutches. You get chemically dependent on any treatment they recommend here in the states. Ibogaine, which is legal in Canada and Mexico, is hard to believe

He didn't bother hiding the EVIDENCE.

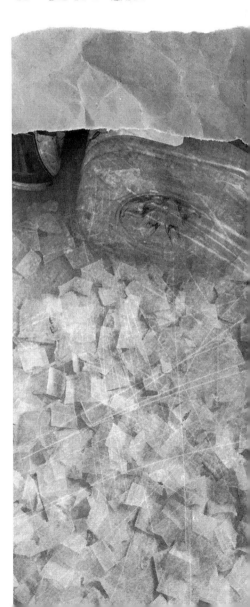

IBOGAINE

PSYCHEDELIC EFFECTS

DEEP TREATMENT

The visions I had from my experience with Ibogaine were life changing.

how effective it is. As far as its psychedelic effects, those are only existent if you take a high enough dose.

When I hallucinated, I watched my funeral, I saw my life in two timelines, Sober and High.

I also dealt with PTSD and resentments. I watched my parents grow old and pass on. I watched myself die in several scenarios. The visions I had from my experience with Ibogaine were life changing.

Some people are discouraged of its psychedelic effects, which is understandable but for me, it was just me laying with a blindfold listening to music that triggered the brain in many ways. My trip was all in black and white. I would see smoke swirling around and turning into things as I watched. My point is, whether you decide you want to engage in deep treatments or not, the fact is, even in micro doses, it COMPLETELY subsides ALL opiate withdrawals. No cold sweats, no shake and aches, no stomach problems, no pain, no anxiety, and depressive episodes. The physical withdrawal from opiates and synthetics are completely eradicated.

Take my word for it, eventually Ibogaine will be legalized after they figure out how to collect even more off addicts. It had to benefit already present facilities because it takes away any need to pay for Subutex, Suboxone or Methadone. I had a therapist who interrupted me at my groups I go to when speaking about Ibogaine, saying it's dangerous and other bullshit.

You know what's dangerous? Uniformed, ignorant people spreading misinformation. During my experience with Ibogaine I had a nurse with me one hundred percent of the time and I had IV fluids as I went into my deep treatment. Basically, what I'm saying to people who have opinions is EDUCATE YOURSELF. We could be detoxing people pain free and focusing on the mental health and mental illness

I saw my life in two timelines, SOBER and HIGH.

He'd surface for quality time with

HIS SON.

aspect of addiction even more so now that the physical withdrawal is NO LONGER a stressful process the addict MUST deal with.

As Dylan's heroin use continued to escalate, he'd occasionally surface for quality time with his son, who was with us four days a week. I discovered the loving memories he made on his phone after his death — a gift for his son to cherish someday.

A substance abuser's first love is their poison, a voice that overpowers and squeezes their heart like a sponge. In Dylan's case, he only left one drip for his son. The perpetually unanswered question was, what do we do now?

The addict's first love is their poison, a voice that overpowers and squeezes their heart like a sponge.

Er's & Psych Wards

Regardless of our children being out of their minds from substance abuse, we cannot get information unless they're lucid enough to sign a disclosure form during hospital admission. Once over age 18, the powers of motherhood are defeated by a federal law, such as HIPPA, that protects the patient's health information.

I was 2,400 miles away in Arizona when a call came from Dylan's friend in NJ. She informed me that he had overdosed and was en route to the emergency room. When I called the nurses' station, an RN clearly defined the HIPAA law. It was *BRUTAL*! My motherhood was outflanked.

A few hours had passed when Dylan's friend called to say the emergency room had discharged him after observation. Dylan returned to the motel we had reserved for him while he awaited a court date.

The following day he called asking for money. When we refused, he became belligerent and threatened suicide, forwarding a text photo of his hand filled with pills. He ceased to answer calls and texts. Unfortunately, I have experienced suicide threats and loss a few times in my life. I don't take them lightly, especially from my child.

My first experience of Dylan's overdose had produced an emotionally heavy toll. Undoubtedly, it was a frothed milk latte of innocence and fear. I had no other choice but to call the police with the motel's address and his car's description. They found Dylan conscious in the parking lot and returned him to the ER.

Once over eighteen, the powers of MOTHERHOOD are defeated.

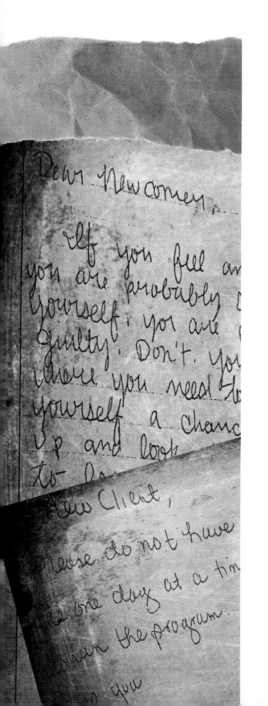

"He's been admitted to psych."

Before heading to the airport, I paced with a raw stomach, aching for answers. Aware that calling the nurses' station would be in vain, I remained a hyper-vigilant mother in distress. Regardless of HIPAA laws, my child was in danger, alone, and needed me. I had nothing to risk in reaching out hoping to snag a soft-hearted soul. I took a deep breath while dialing the nurses' station. When the nurse answered, I begged, as a mother, woman to woman, to please admit my son to the psych ward. I told her that he had threatened suicide, and if he was released, he was likely to die. I heard her slowly take in a deep breath, and upon exhaling, she sighed, "I cannot share any patient information." It was another moment of parental paralysis.

Before boarding my flight, I made one last-ditch call to the nurses' station. At the very most, a nurse could tell me if Dylan was in the ER or discharged. Perhaps my shaken voice and erratic breath gifted me the answer, "He was admitted to psych."

Looking back on the paperwork, the hospital diagnosed him with Mood Disorder/Opioid Dependence. His prescription meds included the following: Clonazepam, Fluoxetine, Quetiapine, and Trazadone. Clonazepam is in the Benzodiazepine class, addictive, and risks dependency; withdrawal can be life-threatening. There's a list of other dangers, especially to a substance abuser who, chances are, will take more than prescribed and could mix with alcohol and other drugs. Fluoxetine, an (SSRI) Selective Serotonin Reuptake Inhibitor: *Can* treat depression and comes with warnings such as some children, teens, and young adults below 25 years of age, had suicidal thoughts during clinical testing.

Next was Quetiapine, which is in a class of medications called atypical antipsychotics. It changes certain natural substances in the brain. There are dozens of potential side effects of this drug. How many of us read all the stapled drug description pages on the pharmacy bag? Before purchasing, we were to check the box to confirm we understood what we were taking, and the pharmacist answered our questions.

Last was Trazadone, a class of medications called serotonin modulators that can treat depression. It works by increasing the amount of serotonin, a natural substance in the brain that helps maintain mental balance. It comes with similar warnings of changes in mental health, and possible suicidal thoughts.

If you have the time, desire, or, as it was in my case, the need to know, there is a wealth of available information that explains exactly how these meds are designed to help regulate the brain's chemistry. There are dozens more with prescription combinations too numerous to list.

From the ER discharge on day one, to the next day's discharge, Dylan was prescribed a new scrip, Seroquel, Prozac, and Klonipin. When he was transferred a couple of days later to a psychiatric hospital, they prescribed Trazadone, Requip, Effexor XR, Buspar, and Remeron with a diagnosis of Major Depressive Disorder. I'm just a mom who has spent endless hours online, reading medical research trials and reports — trying to weave it together to make sense of it all. I understand this was, and is, what most medical and recovery centers offer. Clearly, it's dangerous.

Unsurprisingly, many substance abusers believe by being kept addicted and sick; they help increase profits. I question a doctor's integrity who has the enormous task of providing diagnosis and pharmaceuticals for a substance abuser he's just met. When all else failed, Dylan's scripts seemed to include the popular Seroquel, an antipsychotic which commonly will be backed up with an antidepressant, and a short-time allotment of Klonipin to take the edge off. None of these medicines have proven to cure or heal the mental disorders found in the DSM-5-TR manual.

Each doctor evaluates and prescribes according to their pharmaceutical knowledge from marketing representatives or reading medical journals, many of which are provided

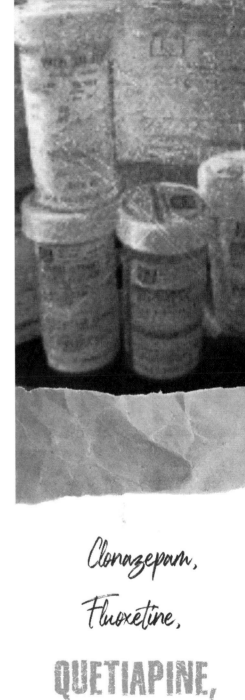

Clonazepam, Fluoxetine, QUETIAPINE, and Trazadone.

None of these medicines have been proven to cure or heal MENTAL disorders.

by Big Pharma. Our loved ones fall victim to this broken science. In one week, the ER, psych ward, and psych hospital had prescribed Dylan three different prescriptions. The psych hospital's diagnosis was major depressive disorder and opioid withdrawal. The discharge meds were mainly for sleep and sedation.

Of course, Dylan couldn't sleep when detoxing. Doctors know this and prefer to comfort the patient rather than risk their relapse. Dylan's brain would start aligning with the meds rather than return to homeostasis. A never-ending battle.

With the intent to remain as numb as possible, Dylan accepted everything prescribed. Each prescription was a non-stick Band-Aid for cravings, sleep, shaky legs, depression, and agitation. I questioned why the doctors didn't focus on or discuss the origin of addiction or the brain's potential for recovery.

Substance abusers are patients who should be under the supervision of a medical doctor who understands addiction, brain chemistry, and medicine. The dosages may need to be changed many times before finding a comfortable combination, and then what? I could not get my son to stay with one doctor. He wanted benzodiazepines like Xanax and, at the time, found a therapist who would prescribe them. Once I saw her name on the medicine bottle, I called to leave her a message. She was young, and easily swayed by my son's charisma. The Xanax would be devoured quickly, snorted up his nose using a dollar bill as a straw.

I learned the term 'off-label," which meant the FDA did not approve it for the specific diagnosis, but a doctor could use his discretion and prescribe if he communicated this to the patient. Would my son with a brain short-circuiting from drug abuse argue or disagree?

Dylan accepted the meds, seldom took them as prescribed, and continued to use heroin and opiates. Doctors cannot be blind to the dangers of prescriptions and substance abusers. Again and again, I begged Dylan to go off everything and give his brain a chance to heal. When he returned home, he chopped and snorted the Clonazepam. His prescribed Lithium was another joke, between his nodding and forgetting to take it on time, and its repercussion of inducing tremors and nausea.

My travels down the psych ward corridors quickly erased the memories of walking hand in hand with my son in the park. The seedy psychiatric hospital looks like a Big Pharma daycare. My eyes shift back and forth, not to stare but peek under each passing hoodie, searching for my baby. No longer could I stick out my lioness' paw when Dylan ventured too far, patting him back to my side.

I almost passed my handsome son, whose blackened eyes denied feeling and expression. His worn beanie stretched over his greasy head of hair. An oversized hoodie dwarfed his tall frame. Oh, how much I detest oversized hoodies and baggy pants.

A doctor approaches us, and he too, is wrung out. The clipboard tucked under his arm is the only thing separating him from the substance abusers. Was it his turn for pro-bono or intern hours? He approached me with a weary look in his eyes. I felt his former altruistic self was as miserable as the walking-dead-eyed substance abusers. Randomly, he opened doors until we found a vacant space.

Dylan and I sat on folding chairs while the doctor flipped through his paperwork. He suggested follow-up care and asked Dylan to initialize. We were handed a copy, pointed to the cashier, and a clerk swiped my card, discharging Dylan. They had it down to the efficiency of a Starbucks drive-through.

Fast-forward five years, Dylan's brain continued to misfire while fed both street and pharmaceutical drugs. During one of our battles, he left the house and forgot to shut off his phone's Snapchat App location. I saw that he was in a neighboring town where we once lived, and his

Each prescription was a non-stick BAND-AID.

friends still resided. Some time passed, and his location was no longer visible.

When it comes to tracking your child, there aren't guarantees of accuracy on their mobile phone. Parents who sign up for family plans, and locator services don't always realize that their child can leave the phone in one location while driving off to another. If only we could microchip them as we do our pets.

Next came a text notification from a friend of Dylan's telling me EMTs had transported him to a behavioral psych hospital. Dylan's social media posts had strong connotations of suicide, and his friend had panicked, calling 911. Suicide was a constant theme in our lives. Every time he was battling withdrawal or messing with his psych meds, he was suicidal. It was painful, exhausting, and always a threat. It can be one of the side effects of substance abuse.

With the precariousness of another failed medical experiment, my imagination crippled me with what lurked within the psych ward's walls. Hour to hour, weighed down by dread, I could not protect my son. I had much doubt that this visit would repair his mental state — another discharge with new scripts, mixed street drugs, and booze.

Dylan was emotionally unavailable when he called, asking me to drop off clean clothing. He shared nothing more. I could never wrap my head around why he would be okay with the lunacy of a psych ward versus trying something holistic. He resisted all my attempts for alternative treatments. Of course, I took it to heart; his dagger often pinned me to the wall.

I entered the dingy corridor, etching a new memory in my tortured soul. An empty security post stood before two wooden doors. The glass peepholes separated me from my son; he would *always* be my baby. Occupying the lobby were vending machines and rotting vinyl chairs. I adjusted my weathered "Mom Cap" while gripping the bag of clothes with Dylan's name printed on masking tape.

There were no instructions, bells, bodies, or help. I called the ward's main number which took me on an air traffic control path. Eventually, I reached an aid on Dylan's floor who told me the security guard was currently in transit with another patient. She told me to leave the clothes by the guard's post. It was a sketchy request, but I felt the need to get out of the building. Hopefully, they would remain until the guard returned.

While placing my bag on the floor, I heard the front door slide open. An older woman entered, followed by a disheveled man in his late 30s, or early '40s. As she guided him toward the lobby, we exchanged glances. She turned toward me, asking if I had spoken with anyone. After explaining my situation, time paused, and our hearts shook hands. She said, "I picked him up from the street. His dad won't let him back. I hope they keep him here." Dipping her head, she turned and walked away. It was clear that she had done more time in addiction-care shackles.

That one hit hard. I was dealing with a 24-year-old, and suddenly I felt fortunate. I hadn't thought it would *never* end, as I continued to hold a vision that Dylan would eventually beat this and live his life.

During the ten-day stay, Dylan's diagnosis and discharge included Bipolar 2 Disorder, Major Depressive Episode, Alcohol Abuse, and Heroin Dependent. It just kept getting better. The doctor was one of the worst, whom I felt should have never been in his position. The prescribed meds for this psych ward trip were Zaleplon, a sleep aid, Clonazepam, addictive benzodiazepine for sedation, Doxepin for depression and anxiety, and Lithium for Bipolar 2.

Psychotic and sedative meds consistently substituted for Dylan's heroin. Did they think this would help? How could someone with extensive training and education allow this to be the prescription for anyone, especially a substance abuser? Would they have prescribed the same for their child?

The glass peepholes separated me from MY SON.

Three days before being admitted to the psych hospital in May 2019, I had asked Dylan to share his thoughts, fears, darkness, and whatever was taunting his consciousness. I had my pen and paper ready.

Small things that no one recognizes is that I left my girlfriend because I knew it would be better for Sobriety. Daily I suffer from suicidal thoughts and manage not to get high, I know it will be my last run. I have constant vignettes, as in driving my car and thinking the world ending. Nuked and the sky is going white, sun burning out and the world ending, random, fucking times. My son is dying all the time and trees going through the window onto his crib. He's bleeding out and choking. When no one is looking, he's finding dad's medicine and choking. I have murder scenarios when in public. It's me doing it and I play it out in my head. What they would say, how I would do it, deal with the body, court process, how much time, murder, suicide. Live in prison the rest of life. Hang myself with a bedsheet. I am figuring out how to get money in prison to OD on heroin. I am always thinking of killing people. If I were in a pissed off mood and someone said something about my language, I would hose my shit, they don't know what is built up in my fucking head. A lot of days, I think that's going to be me. There are people that I'd much rather kill, unfortunately, it will be random person on the wrong day.

Every day, I awake to say, I want to burn this mother-fucker-down. That's the state of mind I'm in. Frustration, anger, and depression. I want to destroy something. That's what I say out loud when waking up. I see myself driving into oncoming traffic, like a truck. Then I see myself going into a field on a blanket in the rain. No one could find me or Narcan me. Or find me for days or weeks. I always wanted to die in the rain. The noose tattoos, Dream 'wood cabin' grass hills, super foggy, pouring rain. I was watching the rain. Out

Psychotic and SEDATIVE meds constantly substituted Dylan's heroin.

He had a
beautiful
heart,
and every now
and then,
he'd share it
with us.

in a fog a silhouette, right before I could see who it was, I woke up.

His intense anxiety is evident in dark thoughts that I've experienced myself. But the more aggressive ones were hard to hear. Dylan existed on two ends of the spectrum. For a young man, he avoided physical confrontations and escaped boyhood fighting. He cared very much for his friends, doing anything possible for them. On the other end of the spectrum, he had dark forces guiding his mental and emotional being, clear evidence of his tortured soul.

Dylan lied, stole, pawned, used, and abused, but was very much loved. He had a beautiful heart, and now and then, it was shared with us. But mostly, with his friends, who he loved and would fiercely protect. Dylan made a difference in the lives of many. Unfortunately, he was born into a world he struggled to live within.

Two weeks after being discharged from the psych hospital, Dylan overdosed. This one was very different from all the others.

I brought him into a world he STRUGGLED to live in.

For the first time, I didn't feel shame or embarrassment over Dylan's overdose, my mom cap and title retracted long ago.

Last Lap

The year 2019 began with failed Methadone, Ibogaine, ERs, outpatient, and psych-ward treatments. After the psych hospital, Dylan had his second to the last overdose. He returned home with his son after a pre-K Father's Day event. One saving grace was that Dylan wouldn't drive impaired, he wanted a clean record.

Within a couple of hours after returning home, the basement door opened, and Dylan's eyes were bulged with an expression of shock. He was incoherent; I ran to grab his arm, so he would not fall down the steps if he lost his balance. I thought he had suffered a stroke, and his actions didn't match previous overdoses. I called my husband, who was outside with my grandson. When they entered the house, I had to dig deep to keep my composure. We guided Dylan safely to the recliner and then called 911.

The EMTs arrived, and as they began unpacking their gear, my mind switched to a prime-time addiction intervention show, with a videographer balancing a camera on his shoulder. While the medics examined Dylan, my grandson tried handing crackers to his daddy. Could this moment ever be worse on an emotional pain-Richter scale? Unfortunately, the answer is yes.

For the first time, I didn't feel shame or embarrassment over Dylan's overdose. This time, I skipped sitting bedside until discharge. Things ballooned so much bigger than me and were out of my hands. My grandson's time was the weekends, and I remained home with my mobile's ringer on full volume.

We guided Dylan safely to the recliner and then called 911.

Constantly,
I thought of
DEATH,
DEATH,
DEATH.

The night passed without a call. While I was getting ready to go to the hospital, my husband received a call from a State Trooper. She told him to pick up Dylan, who was shoeless, five miles from the hospital, and walking down a county highway. When my husband returned with him, I could see something was very wrong with my son. How many times have I had to lose control, fight, and feel incensed?

Still huffing, I called the emergency room, asking, "How is this possible? Where are his discharge papers? Who let him walk out without shoes and transportation?" I knew the routine, and this was an outrage! It was 6:30 a.m. when he began the trek back home. His memory and cognitive skills were absent. I wanted to know what lab tests were ordered and their results. Was he no more than a junkie who needed a good night's sleep? Nothing materialized from 12 hours of hospital tests.

I took Dylan back to the hospital and readmitted him for thousands more dollars for the same blood and urine tests. The psych doctor paid him a visit and read the last two days' bloodwork and urine results, saying only heroin was detected. The doctor explained that Dylan's memory loss could be caused by heroin, and it could eventually lead to Alzheimer's.

I never thought my son's heroin use would lead him to a brain-damaged, vegetative state. Constantly, I thought of *death, death, death* in all its manners and unpleasantries. Dylan's constant of overdose and suicide threats, molded our years of waiting for "*the call.*" As horrific an image it is of your child's passing, it's over. The trade-off is looking into your child's expressionless eyes, wiping drool, and changing diapers forever. Life can be very unkind.

The emergency room psych doctor asked to be alone with Dylan. There was a time that would not be acceptable but beaten down as I was, I closed the curtain and backed out of the room. Not much time passed when the curtain reopened. The doctor avoided eye contact, hanging his

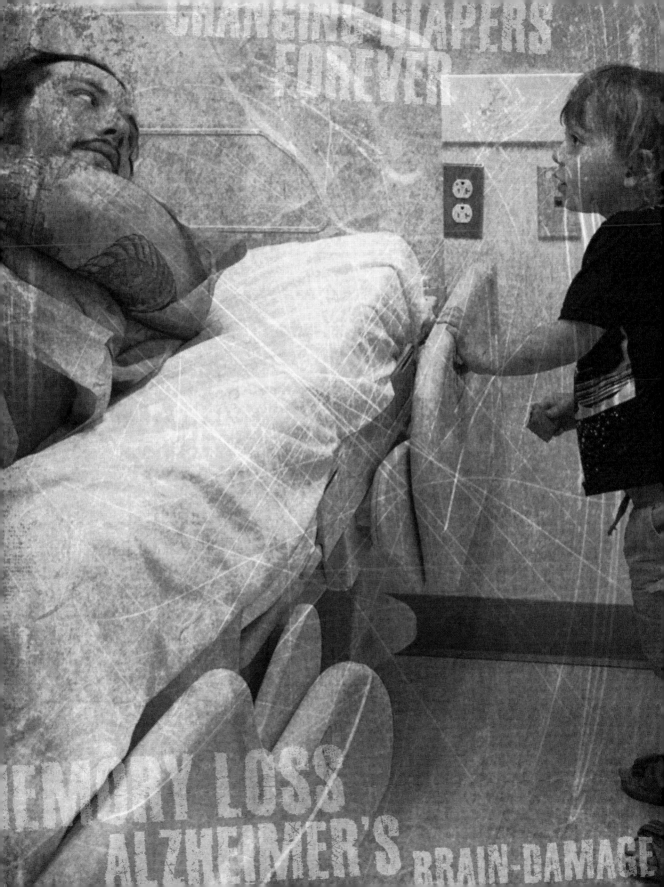

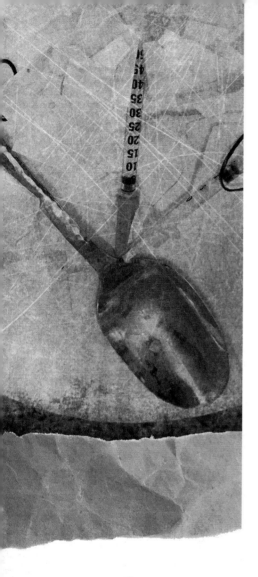

I was pushed
WEAPONLESS
into fear's
battleground.

head low as he passed. The following Monday, Dylan would attend the hospital's outpatient recovery program.

Every attempt at sobriety with Dylan earned me hopeful wings. At the outpatient entrance, I dropped him off, watching him drag his backpack of lunch, drinks, and cigarettes. He'd call when it was over.

Within the hour, my phone lit up, he was ready, and a new nail tapped into my coffin's edge. The moderator asked him to leave because he was challenging authority. Despite Dylan's faults, he stood up for respect and justice. He told me the staff was condescending to the substance abusers, I believed him; he could not hide his defiant, argumentative side. In retrospect, he felt the injustice, but due to the label of *substance abuser*, he hadn't a leg to stand on. It was apparent that we were running out of options. A parent of a substance abuser is hyper-vigilant and prepared for things that generally bring others over the edge. Not to worry, there's no getting dulled down or bored. Down the pike, new treats await.

There was no eye in Dylan's storm; his heroin use peaked, as did the threats to harm us. Trouble brewed when we locked his car keys in a safe. For many reasons we didn't want him driving, including making drug runs to Paterson with an unregistered car. There are few defenses when up against an addict's craving and wrath.

I was pushed weaponless into fear's battleground and standing before me was someone I'd met in a dark alley with little value for life. His need replaced his heart, and at that moment, I feared not death, which wasn't good. I decided to wave the white flag and handed over the keys, instructing him not to return home. No matter how much hurt, hate, and horrible things he did, I'm a mother, not capable of unloving my child. That happens when forced to the brink of emotional fatigue and collapse. Another dreadful day of obsessive thoughts and worry would follow, where is he now?

As nightfall approached, I received a text from one of Dylan's childhood friends, the kind you make during the early years. She was doing her best to keep him with her. All of us were on heightened alert, fearing for his life. Heroin stripped away his remaining life force like a paint thinner. His body, a shell of his former self, was the only identifying particle left. Dylan was no longer there. Helplessness set into my bone marrow like cancer. It constantly hurt.

Around midnight, I heard Dylan knocking on my bedroom window. My mind was tangled in conflict and was incapable of practicing tough love. As much as I wanted to ignore his tapping or keep him sleeping in his car, my heart needed a break. On a dysfunctional level, knowing that he was in the house helped. Indeed, though, it was a double-edged sword.

What does a parent do now? Your child has been in rehab, therapy, medicated, methadone clinics, ibogaine treatment, hospitals, and ERs numerous times. Where do you turn? What else is left? My son's mental health had conjoined with heroin. There would never be a chance of convincing him to accept an alternative approach.

For several years, we have researched addiction-recovery centers. My husband started looking online for help and men's shelters. We needed to get Dylan out of the house for his safety, ours, and his son, who lived with us four days a week.

Remember the pop-up chat window from a few chapters back? The same kind, loving sales rep woman was still working the lines. My innocent husband responded, falling hook, line, and sinker. We never imagined our benefits would cover inpatient treatment, especially with a 25-year-old. Those gals knew how to work the insurance benefits. We put Dylan on a plane, and he entered rehab in a southern state. He willingly left the house, saying, "Thanks for the vacation." He knew his options had run out.

Before I share the rehab's welcome packet, which was charming, I must stress that Dylan was using several bags of heroin daily and was highly volatile. A short stay in

What does a

PARENT

do now?

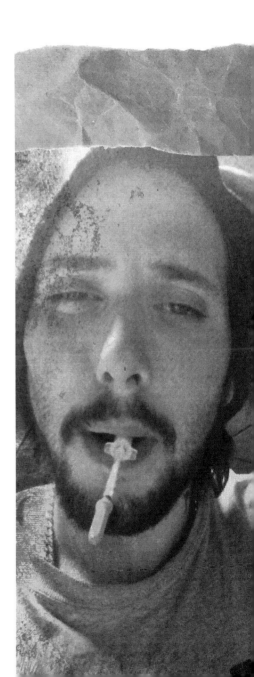

detox and rehab would not heal his brain quickly enough to fulfill the attendance and insurance requirements.

June 24, 2019
Staff:

Your loved one made it to treatment, our program meets seven days per week utilizing modalities of Dialectical Behavior Therapy (DBT), A Balanced Life, Activity Therapy and Psychoeducation. Group topics are based on core components of DBT skills.

And the beat goes on. They had nursing, life skills, and reduction of vulnerability groups. The cream de la crème was in addition to group therapy, participants received weekly individual therapy, case management/discharge planning, nursing care, psychiatric services, medication management, and recovery coaching. The evening schedule included AA/NA/CR (Celebrate Recovery), meetings, evening meditation, and organized social or recreational events.

There wasn't

enough

elixir to

SILENCE

his brain

or rage.

Web-search rehab scams. It will be difficult and uncomfortable at times. I beg all parents to read blogs, vlogs, Facebook, Instagram, and Tick-Tock pages of people in recovery, attending recovery, in addiction, and survivors of rehab addict trafficking. We don't always associate our loved ones with the images presented on these pages. Their stories don't need to mimic ours but read between the lines and see possible patterns.

The good old southern hospitality rehab of Dylan's contract included a *"clients leaving the program"* section. It stated:

Your loved one can leave the program at any time. All treatment is voluntary, although there may be consequences for leaving in certain situations. The intervention team will work to find out why they want to leave early, address any concerns, and attempt to convince them to stay and complete the program. Family member's commitment to the client's continued stay is vital. In our experience, we found that delaying

a client's departure by even a few hours can be the difference between life and death. We want our clients to recover.

The aftercare plan included:

Our clients begin to develop an aftercare plan with their therapy team early in the treatment process and will each receive an aftercare plan specific to their circumstances and situations. Each client has a case manager to help with these transitions. The client's therapist is the first line of contact.

I find it necessary to include contract promises they're unicorns and rainbows. How often in life have you found yourself in the right place, where people want to please you for a reason and endlessly smile until you sign on the dotted line? The rehab's contract included a measurement of safety, and three pages of why things may not turn out for your *loved* one. One of them was called TIB (therapy interfering behavior). I'm guessing that one had Dylan's name etched all over.

TIB's were clients who missed groups, electives, diary card assignments, did not participate in sessions and arrived late to the group. The contract mentioned that the therapists would attempt to identify a specific intervention that could help the client get back on track. A meeting with the clinical director or treatment would be arranged if all else failed. In Dylan's case, none of this came to fruition. There was absolutely no intervention, or client-leaving-the-program support.

Dylan's first week was tough: detoxing, prescribed new meds, and getting caught with a cell phone in his room. His daily reports were not warm and fuzzy. I'm grateful that Dylan signed papers allowing me contact with the staff and therapist. Would he be a candidate for a 30-day graduation ceremony in another three weeks?

By the end of the second week, I began to feel anxious. Dylan's therapist was not a good match, and soon he'd be assigned a new one. In the meantime, the therapist called

me with difficult questions and reported his conflicts with Dylan. I've read about trauma and addiction, but I don't know of Dylan experiencing any. Those specializing in the trauma and addiction believe there is no doubt a connection. Dylan did admit to experiencing post-traumatic stress disorder from the hood when held up by gunpoint and another time when he witnessed a child thrown from a vehicle during a car accident.

The loud clicking of the 30-day clock added to my stress, along with Dylan's pending N.J. traffic violation and court date. Luckily, his attendance in rehab enabled me to take care of the fine. I worried if he left rehab prematurely, would he have to face the court date? My stomach knotted when the phone rang with the rehab's area code. I anticipated that Dylan had left, got into a fight, told off the therapist, or put his fist through a wall. After every storm, the sun will shine, but in the case of drug addiction and rehab, there's no guarantee of an outcome. If hope were the energy of all loving families, it could power the world.

When the rehab restored Dylan's phone privileges, he'd call for a quick chat asking for a cash transfer to his debit card. I told him to take off the Scarface persona, his above-everyone bullshit, and take a good look in the mirror. His support was thinning and in his corner of the ring, dangling over the rope, was a dirty towel and empty water bottle. It was painful, and my deepest fear was losing him: misery's last vision is a horror for any family. Generally, Dylan's disobedience was fueled by what he saw as unethical practices, disrespect for patients, and other humanitarian causes.

According to the therapist, Dylan wasn't attempting to work the program. I assumed he was his usual depressed and angry self. At the time, I never lived in the present moment, and constantly worried about tomorrow. The following email reflects the rehab's decision, made halfway through the month.

If hope were the energy of all the LOVING families, it could power the world.

The
THERAPIST,

who was no match

for Dylan,

was not

reassigned.

July 11, 2019
Rehab staff email:

> *Good morning, at this point, Dylan is not appropriate for outpatient care. Going to the next level down is not an option, right now.*

Me:

> *Can you please clarify. The next level down is outpatient? If at the end of the month he is not a candidate for aftercare or outpatient, what is recommended?*

Staff:

> *Our next level down would be Next Step, which is intensive outpatient, which he is not a candidate for. Same routine as inpatient care but living in a house with other guys but still expected to attend groups. Right now, Dylan is not participating. If Dylan stayed here, he would be referred to an IOP and housing or an extended care program. Sober living would not be treated the same as inpatient care or IOP care. An IOP would still show that he is seeking treatment but if he does not go to the meetings or groups, it would be documented. Legally, not attending groups and meetings is not good. The courts can ask for records to show participation.*

Me:

> *Is he not attending meetings?*

Staff:

> *He has been refusing to participate and attend groups.*

Me:

> *I'll talk to his therapist today. I want to be able to talk with Dylan as well, if allowed. He doesn't realize that this is his last stop. There is no coming back. I need to tell him that.*

Staff:

> I completely understand your position and will pass a message to his therapist.

Me:

> Yes, please pass that on, time is running out and I'm trying to do some prevention. Dylan thinks the same will repeat, and it's not going to.

At times like these, we can become frustrated and angry at our child; no doubt I did. When desperation sets in, it can be overwhelming. But how much of this can be placed on our child? Why didn't anyone reach out and explain what the hell was really happening?

What meds was Dylan placed on, and were they changed throughout the month? Where was the rehab's dynamic medical and psychological staff? Dylan was ill, and no one contacted me with where I could seek medical advice. My confusion peaked when the therapist said Dylan was somewhat surrendering. I was hopeful and reached out with another email.

July 19, 2019, 8:35 am
Me:

> Can you let me know the status of Dylan's case? Will he be continuing there/next level? I have a package that I wanted to mail and double check before doing so.

9:04 am
Staff:

> I forwarded your email to Dylan's therapist. I have no way of knowing if he will go to the Next Step. That is a clinical/medical decision.

9:05 am
Me:

> OK, can you please give me his therapist's email?

My heart soon cooled when Dylan's "aftercare" plan exit did not include the contract's therapy teams, case managers, and support back into society. That's an offer

The 30 days were up, and Dylan was too much work.

Jul 19, 2019, 2:28 PM

I'm trying to figure out where to go

They have a van out front ready to drop me at a bus stop

I will fuckung go ballistic right now. I already wrote case mgmt. u stay there until we make the plan. They can call me if they have a problem, Start checking sober houses

This place is so fucked up

My friend in Cali May have a sober living I can go to and I asked my friends in FL of my insurance will work

received from the behaved, cooperative, quietly medicated clients. My son's exit came abruptly.

Dylan's therapist passed him in the hall on the day of the moving-up ceremony and dropped the bomb, "Today, we are discharging you." Dylan was surprised, and I was confused. The therapist had told me that Dylan was somewhat surrendering two days prior.

What did I miss? I didn't see this coming and had only received an hour's notice before discharge. I felt the staff had decided on their morning coffee break. The 30 days were up, and Dylan was too much work.

We were several states away, and I needed to arrange transportation to the airport, air travel, transfer money, and plan where Dylan was going next. He needed to continue recovery support. Coming home would sabotage his only chances. My last email:

Me:

> *I got the heads-up about Dylan's discharge. What I need to express is contacting a parent an hour before discharge is awful! I spoke with Dylan's therapist two days ago and was told that Dylan was somewhat surrendering. I ended the conversation expressing that I was hopeful he would make it to the Next Step. OK, so Dylan doesn't earn the stripes for the Next Step, so be it, but the way this was handled is again, awful! Parents such as us need to find Dylan a place to go other than his home. This was clearly communicated over the past four weeks. Now Dylan's phone is apparently lost, and we need to find another resource asap.*
>
> *Please make a note of this and pass it on to whoever can possibly help in a situation like ours in the future. I'm infuriated. Not because Dylan didn't make it, but because I had NO notice other than an hour. Dylan may not have been the greatest of patients, but he could be correct about the lack of professionalism of your clinic.*

Dylan not making the next step to outpatient did not upset me; he wasn't easy. But one thing was for sure: true to his being, he stood for truth and fought incompetent authority figures when justified. It seemed that Dylan was no match for anyone. The doctors never consulted about the medications they administered. The center's medicinal cocktail may have quickly subdued other clients, but Dylan wasn't one of them. When he left New Jersey for this rehab center four weeks prior, he was combative, put through detox, and received a new prescription of meds. He was there *one week* when I received the email that said he would not move up to outpatient status at the end of the month. One week, and there was no hope? One week, and he was detoxed with a healthy, rewired brain? What were his chances? I regret not knowing then what I know today. I would never have sent him to another addiction-recovery center.

During the frenzy on discharge day, Dylan hooked up with someone who referred him to a recovery center in Los Angeles, CA. In *desperate parent* mode, my husband and I secured Dylan's travel arrangements to California. I had no information and was at the mercy of Dylan, and an unknown source, who guaranteed that Dylan would be admitted, and our insurance was approved.

A few days passed; I hadn't heard anything from Dylan. I kept the previous texts from the mystery source and sent a message asking where my son was. The anonymous person said he was admitted but would not have phone privileges for the first two weeks. It was now July 2019.

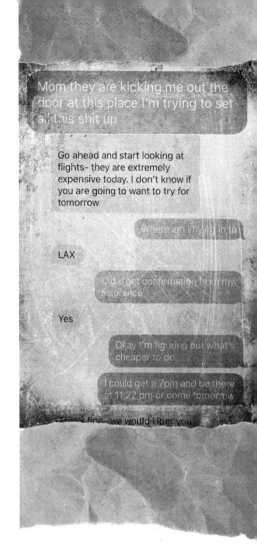

Mom they are kicking me out the door at this place I'm trying to set all this shit up

Go ahead and start looking at flights- they are extremely expensive today. I don't know if you are going to want to try for tomorrow

Where am I flying in to

LAX

Did I get confirmation from my insurance

Yes

Okay I'm figuring out what's cheaper to do

I could get a 7pm and be there at 11:22 pm or come tomorrow

That's fine, we would Uber you

One week, and there was no **HOPE?**

It can hit hard when faced
with the realization that
rose-colored glasses have
smudge marks.

8

Sobriety & Pink Clouds

When the detox lockdown passed, Dylan called, saying he liked California, his sober house, and the IOP center. The sober house granted some freedom, allowing him to venture outdoors. He even met with old NJ friends who had relocated to the West Coast. For the first time, he seemed agreeable and in a good way. The housemates were working on their sobriety, and everyone seemed to resonate and be supportive. That gal *hope* started knocking on my door. She'd been trouble in the past, especially when Dylan texted dark-humored cartoons. My heart would temporarily lift, and I'd forgo the fantasy of walking by the river with a pocket filled with rocks.

There's little doubt that when in early recovery, one is vulnerable to life's challenges. Dylan's was being a chick magnet in a co-ed sober house. It didn't take long before he emotionally bonded with one of the girls, and within two weeks, he was riddled with heartache. I felt his pain when he called to tell me she had relapsed on Fentanyl-laced Xanax, overdosed, and died. He had lost a friend back home to overdose the same week.

My heart hurt for Dylan, the beautiful girl whose life was taken so young, and for her parent's unfathomable pain. They sent their daughter across the country in good faith to be saved, not returned in a body bag. These are some of the possible scenarios, heartbreaking tales, of attending addiction-recovery centers.

Dylan's back-to-back loss of friends from overdose, broke him enough to relapse with alcohol, and be placed into detox. After detox, he returned to his sober house, and IOP meetings.

That gal
HOPE
started
knocking
on my door.

My tattered

HEART

was scarred,

but not enough

to avoid the joy of

hearing my son

speak of hope,

plans, and a

future.

For over 90 days, Dylan was drug-free or *clean* as they say. He transitioned into the *pink cloud* stage. This term, coined by AA (*Alcoholics Anonymous*), represents a temporary joy and elation. The pink cloud doesn't have a specific beginning or end, but does end. There's a sense of excitement, and an urgency to do all you've missed. Feeling that good can sidetrack you to work still ahead and doesn't mean your sober work is close to complete. That's the negative side of the pink cloud; waking up and realizing the rose-colored glasses have smudge marks is hard.

When my son entered his pink cloud, I felt we were meeting for the first time. With an empty toolbox, Dylan braved embracing a decade's worth of trapped and repressed feelings of pain, love, and regret. His vulnerable, authentic self suddenly lusted for life. My tattered heart was scarred, but not enough to avoid the joy of hearing my son speak of hope, plans, and a future. I don't know if there's a normal, but this was the closest I'd ever felt. His voice, words, and inflection returned to normal, dropping most of the slang from the hood. Here are some of his writings when at his best.

Oct 16,

> Most of my life I've not had faith in humanity, believing people will just consume and decay until the earth gets hit with an asteroid or we end from nuclear war. The birth of my son gave me purpose to stay alive, but I still suffered in silence with my vices. It has been a hell of a journey these twenty-five years, but just now in my life, I've been experiencing the beautiful side of humanity. Whether it's kindness to strangers or belly laughs with good friends. There is a pocket of happiness amongst this mess we call earth. I've seen so many people die, it has changed my perspective on life, and I do genuinely appreciate still being alive. I probably shouldn't be here but I'm here. Life goes by too fast.
>
> I Love seeing my son grow-up. He is so bright and innocent, he makes me a better person. I no

"The birth of my son gave me the purpose to stay alive."

longer chase death carelessly gambling with my life playing Russian roulette. Just recently I genuinely believe if you put positive energy out you will receive it back. I've had some ridiculous coincidences since I've taken this approach, so I will continue to do so. Anyway, that's my two cent Tuesday.

Nov 3, 2019

Being broken down and hurt to a point of desperation and fierce anger & animosity can be extremely humbling once you realize you can embrace and feel that emotion without numbing it with drugs or alcohol. After being in a constant loop for so many years where you are doing exactly that, it is dangerous and triggering when dealing with such situations. But once you realize you are at a counterpoint in your life where you can deal with life without using a crutch, you feel humbled, empowered, and morally and emotionally strong. I've had a few close calls since I got sober, especially recently, but I will continue to cut out the deadweight, shitty friends, and toxic people in my life. I'm doing so well; I don't need these people in my life. It's time to grow, spiritually, emotionally, mentally, and physically. So Imma say it one time If you ever took advantage of me or took my kindness and friendship for granted, Go fuck yourself.

Nov 2019 Thanksgiving

I'm thankful for my son, I'm thankful for those who believe in me and haven't given up on me. I'm thankful for the men I consider brothers, and women I consider sisters. I'm thankful for the military out fighting so we can enjoy this day. I'm thankful for my team out here in Cali who help me in sobriety. I'm thankful to be sober almost half a year!! I am so thankful for my parents for never giving up on me and doing so much for me so I could have a

He wanted to become an

ADVOCATE

and educate the substance abuser's plight.

chance and make it this far. I'm thankful to my son's mother for understanding why I must be across the country for now working on myself. And finally, I am thankful for all of you, sometimes the only thing that gets me thru the day is being sober till the next day ... I have people I know on my Facebook, and I have people I've met thru meme groups, either way when I make posts and get support or feedback it really makes my heart warm. I appreciate those who engage in my 100% honest type of mindset, and I've had more support on the Internet then I've had in real life, so I want to send all of you love and gratefulness I hope everyone enjoys their day. Please keep in mind the families who have lost their sons daughters sister brother mom dads from addiction. I am blessed to be able to tell you all I love you today.

We finally surfaced from years of turbulent seas. I was emotional and loved who Dylan was, and he had always been. Many of the people we pass living under cardboard are also beautiful souls. Unfortunately, they did not receive an opportunity to be awakened, or perhaps their family gave up.

Dylan spoke about his life, plans, and son. He wanted to become an advocate and educate the substance abuser's plight. It was a time to remove the stigma from an addict, and his family and burn down the curtain of pride. As much of a gift Dylan's awakening was, it would also serve as a curse when taken away. It reminded me of the movie *The Awakenings* with Robert DeNiro and Robin Williams. DeNiro's character is reawakened by a test drug, only to return to his former immobile self. Within one month of the pink cloud stage, I lost my hope-filled loving son once again, to the dark side.

DETOX HOPE-STRUGGLE

In early recovery, one is vulnerable to life's changes

D-Day

Dylan's struggles began with the constant change of scripts, dosages, and not receiving meds in a timely manner. While attending an IOP meeting, he witnessed the FBI raiding the premises. He also observed substance abusers trafficked for a price tag to relapse and reenter the detox phase.

As for his sober house, some of his roommates needed more psychological support. It was unsettling to be sharing a home with someone slamming cabinets, talking to themselves, and acting what he'd call *batshit crazy*. I had read of these accounts online; you can view them by web searching rehab scams. Some rehabs accept patients *'for insurance benefits,'* who are suffering from other mental disorders other than substance abuse.

The sober house managers, recovering substance abusers, were also working on their sobriety. They had their hands full with willful, recovering roomies, who had to behold a chore list: Whose turn was it to clean the bathroom, empty the dishwasher, or clean the kitchen? Who didn't show up to IOP, house meeting, and whose urine tested positive? House managers were responsible for dispensing the prescription meds and had their phones blowing up all day.

During the hectic, day-to-day madness of who has an extra cigarette, pill, and food-card money, Dylan focused maintaining sobriety each minute of the hour, and day. The remaining hours were exhausted with the others who shared life's misery.

Dylan's pill list included meds for anxiety, muscle spasms, focus, pain, sleep, staying awake, depression, and

House managers were responsible for dispensing the PRESCRIPTION meds and had their phones blowing up all day.

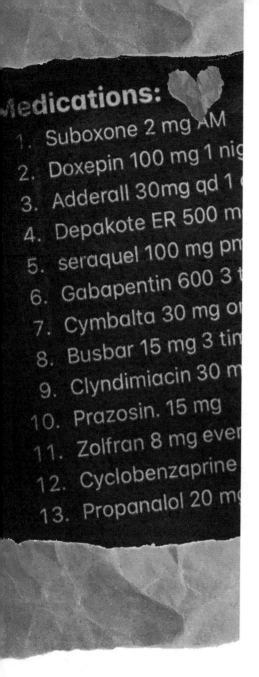

Medications:

1. Suboxone 2 mg AM
2. Doxepin 100 mg 1 nig
3. Adderall 30mg qd 1
4. Depakote ER 500 m
5. seraquel 100 mg pn
6. Gabapentin 600 3 t
7. Cymbalta 30 mg o
8. Busbar 15 mg 3 tin
9. Clyndimiacin 30 m
10. Prazosin. 15 mg
11. Zolfran 8 mg ever
12. Cyclobenzaprine
13. Propanalol 20 m

I learned the term

POLYPHARMACY

withdrawal management. He met with his doctor weekly to discuss the medication's side effects, while trying to find the right combination to ease his angst. Nothing worked, Dylan was constantly agitated and frustrated. He was slowly deteriorating.

I believe those struggling with substance abuse, withdrawal, and who are heavily medicated should be under constant supervision, be it by a trained professional or loved ones. Living amongst a group of substance abusers all in early recovery, who are being managed by an untrained staff member in recovery, is not a match for success and healing. The following is Dylan's last med list from rehab.

Suboxone	2 mg – am
Doxepin	100 mg pm
Adderall	30 mg am
Depakote ER	500 mg -250 mg 2x day
Seroquel	100 mg pm
Gabapentin	600 mg – 3x day
Cymbalta	30 mg 1x day
Busbar	15 mg 3x day
Clindamycin	30 mg – 7 days
Prazosin	15 mg
Zofran	8 mg every 6 hours
Cyclobenzaprine	10 mg
Propranolol	20 mg as needed

I learned the term "polypharmacy," which, in essence, means to test, discuss side effects and new dosages, and retest again and again. There is a risk, as with anything, of sickness, relapse, or death. If you look at the above med list, you should feel the chill.

Science is not a quick fix, and it will take many more lab mice, rats, and human clinical testing before we have answers.

I discovered numerous text messages between Dylan, sober house managers, and IOP staff, relating to his issues of missing meds. Often, he was in short supply or without medication for a few days. The IOP's doctor prescribed

SICKNESS RELAPSE DEATH IS A RISK

If you look at the list,
you should feel the chill.

meds, a pharmacy delivered them to his sober house, and a house manager dispensed them.

The following text exchanges represent what brought about the inevitable downfall, and December 5, 2019, discharge. Dylan was in terrible shape, and his rage clearly escalating. Especially when the sober house decided to downgrade him to OP (outpatient.) That meant if he remained in the house, his rent responsibility would be $2,000 a month. The prescription disasters, brain imbalance, unaddressed reasons for addiction, and added pressures on his nervous system, doomed him to fail.

November 22, 2019

DYLAN: *I appreciate the help and I'm trying not to step on anyone's toes. I didn't expect you guys to pull my meds out of your asses. I don't know why Harry felt like I was putting pressure on you guys. I just wanted to make sure I had everything written down. My family and I know I gotta stay out here until I get my shit together because I won't have this opportunity again. Especially losing the insurance. I may not be getting high but I'm really struggling still. I need to pursue that EMDR and psychiatrist and everything. My head's seriously fucked. But I just wanted to apologize to you guys, I wasn't trying to use or annoy you guys. Was just trying to put all those meds in one place so they can be one less thing I can worry about.*

IOP: *No worries or apologies necessary. We are here to help you figure things out. Let's sit and get all written down and get some organization so it's streamlined and not overwhelming.*

November 30, 2019

Dylan: *Embarrassingly woke up my roommate whimpering and shit because I'm out of Prazosin. Hope I get things taken care of Monday. I'm out of a bunch of meds.*

IOP: Oh, no I'm sorry your struggling, this is why I wanted you to bring in all meds from any/all Drs, bring in Monday.

Dylan: Sorry for texting u directly. I'll be bringing my meds and finding out about emdr.

December 1, 2019

Dylan: Did I get my meds this morning? I can't remember I keep falling asleep from these meds.

SH: Nah, u gotta come get them you're starting OP tomorrow.

December 3, 2019

Dylan: Any word on medications there?
          I don't understand how this place can put you on medication for your brain and not be able to make sure you don't detox from it. It's been days and they went and told me to fuck myself again. It's unbelievable.

Dylan: They just got here without my fucking medication. With the way this fucking bullshit is going, I'll just relapse and u can hit my fucking insurance again because I'm sick of this.

IOP: This is why you should have a sponsor, so you have someone to talk to.

Dylan: Yup, so that way when my sober house pushes me to OP, holds rent over my head and doesn't give me my medication AND says they don't trust me with my sleep meds I have someone to talk to. I have a sponsor.

Dylan: I've just been in a shit place mentally recently. It's been hard to get out of this headspace I don't know if it's A little medication, which by the way, I had been trying to get My meds since before Thanksgiving but I'm missing a bunch and I ran out of my adhd medicine which chemically is close to Methamphetamine so you may see me really tired or short fused, anger problems just

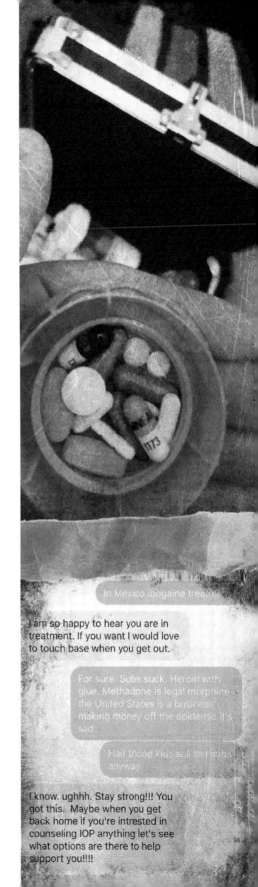

know it's very possible I may be reacting to not having that med.

Dec 3, 2019

SH: *Your Meds are supposed to be delivered today.*

Dylan: *I spoke to James, hopefully he's bringing them. I'm detoxing currently, it's not fun.*

SH: *Do you need any other meds besides the Gabapentin 800 mg and the Adderall?*

Dylan: *Yeah, a fucking Xanax would be solid. I've already spoke to the doctor, I'm sure he was going to increase the dose, but I didn't go in today so I didn't have a chance to. I'm a twenty-five-year-old man, who has been pretty good here. Besides being a little messy, I'm not that bad of a housemate. I haven't relapsed and done shady shit. If it was a problem, I took an extra Seroquel if I couldn't sleep, then take them, I don't care. It's not a big deal. I don't try and get high off my meds. I just want to function.*

SH: *The Adderall will be sent to the Rite Aid where you normally go, it should be ready tonight. But I'd call before you go to be sure they're ready.*

Dylan: *Where is the Rite Aid, Near the weed place, across from Starbucks?*

SH: *I don't know, I'm literally repeating what IOP said and the pharmacy you normally use I assume.*

Dylan: *They always deliver it, so I have no clue.*

SH: *OK, hold on, I'll see*

Dylan: *I'm gonna go ahead and guess I'm fucked for meds today. IOP never got back to me. If anything changes, please let me know.*

My conversations with Dylan had felt like tightened twist-ties on the wrists, but now I know why. I was familiar with his angry, cursing verbal abuse; the only time he slurred was when using alcohol or heroin. Hearing him slur from the sober house was upsetting. At first, I thought he was using, but learned it had been the lack of and combination of meds

I haunted Dylan to share the scripts and dosages, regardless of how often they changed. I regret not fighting harder to get answers. It all happened quickly in the end. I'd ask him to hand the phone over to staff or medical personnel each time we spoke, and there was always an excuse why it wasn't possible. No one called me, and I didn't have a contact number. An impossible situation with a child over 18.

The insurance statement showed $503.00 daily, coding it as a hospital room. There were weekly charges of $1,500-$3,000 per lab testing. It didn't add up, and I asked Dylan how this was possible and what they were testing, and his reply was "urine."

The doctors didn't invest a personal interest in my son. Their job was to medicate him enough to behave, participate in IOP, relieve withdrawal symptoms, and meet insurance requirements. Dylan's doctor added a prescription for ADHD meds to keep him awake during the IOP meetings. The prescribed meds in his system kept him from sleeping and staying awake. He would lie on the floor during the IOP meetings. There were messages with the IOP staff and his sober house managers, suspecting him of using drugs. He was repeatedly tested and came out negative. The doctors bombarded his system with pharmaceuticals, and Dylan started to lose his grasp and clarity but remained sober. While writing this book, I consulted with a pharmacist who said the Adderall should not have been prescribed with some of the other medication.

The day arrived when Dylan's sober house management discharged him, basically kicked him out. He was experiencing withdrawal symptoms from missing meds, argumentative, and voiced his opinion on insurance scams and addict trafficking. He used it as ammunition against the staff who demanded the $2,000 in rent.

After being at the sober house from July through December, with one relapse on alcohol, he became

No one called me.

I didn't have a contact number.

Insurance was billed $503.00 daily.

There were weekly charges close to $1500.00-$3000.00 for lab testing.

It didn't add up.

Dylan Cole
November 4 · 👥

Feel the bass

Finally made a beat that is the same caliber as my old ones. Music is my best outlet for emotion.

OVERDOSE

12:57 ↗

◖◗ LTE

< Dylan Cole ▶ Addiction Recovery
Friday at 1:41 PM · 🌐

30 days no heroin mothafuckaaa
👍👍👍👍 😊

YOUTUBE.COM
ColdSoulCole - Overdose

homeless in Los Angeles. We learned about it when he posted a video on social media. He was on a corner with his possessions stuffed in garbage bags. Immediately we were faced with the arduous task of finding Dylan a place to stay while unbeknownst to us, he was wheeling and dealing with the scamming referral agents.

We could not reserve a hotel room by phone with a credit card, and cash was not an acceptable payment. Expedia would work until he'd arrive without a credit card to show. We kept Dylan riding around town in an Uber while his phone battery was dying. The stressors were insurmountable. Finally, a previous sober house roomie allowed him to recharge in her car.

I dreaded transferring cash to his debit card but didn't have a choice. He needed to eat. Eventually, I found a motel in a seedy side of town willing to accept my credit card. At least Dylan would have a roof over his head.

Instant Karma: payback was immediate. In a couple of hours, he posted bar photos with a drink in hand on his social media. He partied with a former sober house roomie while bargaining with the referral agents who promised the highest bounty for his head.

A referral agent established a payout for Dylan, leading to a new detox and recovery program. The longer he stayed, the more money made. I didn't have contact information for the agent or the recovery center. It wouldn't be until our insurance company sent paperwork home that I would know the recovery center's name. By then, Dylan had finished the agreed two weeks and was trafficked to another detox facility. I pieced it together through Dylan's text messages.

I was fortunate to find a hotel manager who would accept cash with a deposit. I didn't know Dylan was clearing his system of drugs and alcohol between placements. That's what the substance abuser will do, and it's incredibly dangerous due to them being sober for a while. Many will lose their lives by overdose while being trafficked.

He

PARTIED

with a former

sober house roomie

while bargaining with

the referral agents

who promised the

highest bounty

for his head.

The truth about the recovery-world FRAUD *operations.*

Dylan's last referral took him into late January 2020, where he remained except for the week before returning home. Our credit-card statement reflected dozens of Uber charges we later learned were for delivering food and alcohol.

During the revision stage of this book, I was providing a resource section and came upon a movie I'd never watched. After reading the reviews, I purchased and watched it through Prime video. The 2021 movie is called *Body Brokers,* written, and directed by John Schwab. The movie is a true story based on John's experience. It's a must-watch movie for anyone contemplating sending their child to a recovery center. It's a good part of what happened to my son, and depicts the truth about the recovery-world industry and its multi-billion-dollar fraud operations. The next chapter is how it worked with Dylan.

The **FBI** raided his **ICP** center.

10
Trafficking Substance Abusers

In this book's introduction, I mentioned that substance abusers and frightened parents were big businesses. It is analogous to thirsty referral agents fusing with multi-level salespeople who'd sell their mother for a buck. The pumped adrenalin rush comes from payout bonuses of pushing people instead of drugs. Here we switch from drug dealer to addict broker.

During Dylan's pink cloud stage, the FBI raided his IOP center. He sent video footage of agents carrying out boxes, files, and electronic equipment. He said the other agents were inside, searching the ceilings of offices. I asked what he thought was up, and he said:

> "Possible insurance fraud and shit like paying people to relapse, go through detox and start their insurance charges from the beginning. Usually, young kids who don't want to stay sober will go into detox. Then their insurance is charged for PHP, then IOP; switching to a brother clinic, and doing the same, would be a good way to make money back. The IOP is the middleman with druggies and insurance. They are looking for fraudulent insurance charges on the computers and files about clients moved around, chronic relapsers, and shit. It sucks because it was alright going for the group, and I liked the people, but they were cashing in on people, marketing their insurances, and secluding and investigating employees."

Agents were carrying out boxes, files, and electronic

EQUIPMENT.

198

Days

9
Hours

48
Minutes

58
Seconds

Since Heroina

● ● ●

Pushing Dylan to make a deal,

QUICK CASH

if he'd relapse.

Reading through Dylan's texts, I discovered his connection to a referral agent from our neck of the woods. In June, when the southern rehab had discharged Dylan with an hour's notice, this agent worked his magic. We had Dylan landing in California and admitted into a detox center within a few hours. At the time, it felt like a gift. Dylan's text messages reflected that a bonus check was in his future. Regardless of the bonus, he still would have partaken in the recovery center.

Due to the FBI raiding Dylan's IOP center, there would not be a bonus payout. The referral agent said, '*due to unforeseen circumstances,*' but in good faith, threw Dylan a bone taking a couple of hundred dollars out of his own pocket. Not even close to the expected payout, but something. I saw the $200 deposited in Dylan's bank account with the agent's name on record.

For the next few months other headhunters had their eyes on Dylan. One repeatedly appeared in the text messages, preying upon Dylan to relapse for a cash deal. Their shared texts revealed Dylan's contentment with his current sober house, roommates, and that he didn't want to change. Of course, it didn't last when the agent casted a line '*large payout for relapse*' during what I called, Dylan's '*perfect storm.*'

Dylan was becoming vulnerable, and struggling with missing his son, birthdays, and experiencing serious drama with old acquaintances back home. This sequence of events joined force with the sober house managers forcing employment, two thousand a month rent, and Dylan's ongoing prescription issues. I noticed his tone changed; frustration and anger began to resurface. When the managers asked for my phone number to discuss the rent, Dylan's fly-off-the-handle rage, told me they were scamming our insurance.

Suddenly, Dylan's sober house was no longer suitable. They told him he had been part of a scholarship. I'll never know what went down. It began as a referral, and HIPPA laws kept me in the dark. I don't know what insurance paid,

I did report my findings a few months after Dylan's death, suggesting an investigation.

Dylan's text messages included conversations with someone of rank in his IOP and he promised to not name the employee but shared that he witnessed trafficking. During this time, he was spiraling downward. However, I didn't know the reason until after his death.

For years, substance abusers have been sold and resold to addiction-recovery centers. It can also be an inside job from the facilities staff. Do some online research, and you'll find more evidence of the rehabs exchanging bodies for bonuses. They keep the addict in the system with slight adjustments to the sober house. Our children risk overdosing when passed between recovery centers. They know they'll be reentering detox, so they might as well enjoy some substances or alcohol before going back.

There's so much that will and can go wrong. Again, do your homework and READ everything you can find online! The following are unedited text exchanges between my son and referral agents, which reflect how the game is played.

BILL: *OK, you're approved and good to come today, can't wait to see you, I'll pick you up at the airport. I work there and asked if I can bring you and they said cool.*

DYLAN: *What do you do there, and what's the housing like?*

BILL: *I do a bunch of random stuff for the company, I drive and help people get to and from the facility. I know the program well. It's a good spot, just don't act like a fool man let's get your life together.*

Little by little, the agent starts to backpedal. When he's about to scoop Dylan from the airport, he discovers his car headlight is out. He orders Dylan an Uber, and then learns he can't get Dylan admitted into his sober house, so he placed him in one which was an hour and a half away.

Scumbag

DYLAN: How much you make sending me here? You should throw me some bread for cigs. I'm broke out here, and you made a bunch of bread.

BILL: Bro, u just got there hang tight for a lil. Call me when you are back and alone.

DYLAN: How much u make off me, I might have someone I can get here.

BILL: Send their info and I'll call you bout that.

DYLAN: How much do you usually make off people?

BILL: Depends on insurance.

DYLAN: He's in Virginia but he will come out here. What did u make off my blue cross blue shield?

BILL: Bro, nothing yet I told u this the other day. Can we chill on texting this and can u do me a favor and delete our texts?

DYLAN: Yeah bro what you think someone gonna go thru my phone?

BILL: Yeah I do cuz they do that at these places like another week and we break bread on u homie. It's all good, I'm just paranoid.

DYLAN: Why is it illegal?

BILL: BROOOOOO

DYLAN: I'll delete the texts if you're really worried.

BILL: I am, LOL call me! We can talk on the phone.

DYLAN: So, I heard how this deal goes now.

BILL: Bro I bet, I can talk a lil later. U free around 5?

Next, is a text of the IOP center when raided by the FBI. It appears he never met up with Dylan or had a private call. Sometimes there is a delay in hours or days in exchanging texts with Dylan and the referral agent.

DYLAN: People behind the curtains over here at the center. We got raided by the FBI bro LOL

BILL: Yeah, I know, this shit is wild as fuck.

DYLAN: I been keeping my head down. Told some friends who work here to do the same. Don't ask questions and they'll be fine.

Do me
a favor
DELETE
our texts.

I didn't get paid on u the spot got RAIDED.

BILL: *Shit is creepy though. Got some beds open at this spot for detox rez.*

DYLAN: *Where's the bread?*

BILL: *No one talked to me from the IOP, I don't know what the fuck is goin on.*

DYLAN: *They are slipping dog, so sketch.*

BILL: *They apparently did this to everyone that worked there.*

Bill began to coax Dylan into switching sober houses. In November, Dylan gave Bill insurance information but never followed up. When Dylan left the rehab on December 5, 2019, he was trafficked and placed in a two-week detox. Afterward, he contacted Bill, who put him up for a day in his house before placing Dylan in the second detox. During this time, Dylan began to bottom out mentally and emotionally and told me he was going to relapse for a payout, and all he had to do was use his prescribed meds with alcohol. To make the payout worth it, you had to remain in detox for a minimum of 14 days. The longer Dylan stayed, the larger the bonus.

DYLAN: *So, the place u sent me raped my insurance to the ground and getting audited.*

BILL: *That's not how insurance works bro, why do you think that? your shit resets January 1st.*

DYLAN: *Sucks that u used me as a dummy. Now that I know wassup people offering so much money. Surprised that who I met here is kickin me bread more than my jersey homies.*

BILL: *I didn't, it got raided, I used that place a lot beforehand. U have a plan that uses in network rates only, so it's tough to even place you*

DYLAN: *Hope those bitches were fuckin wit get locked. I was way off PHP (partial hospitalization program) by then.*

BILL: *U were only there for sober living. That's the lowest paying level of care too, so if u just did detox rez and got some money for it cool. But you ain't hit me up trying to make money after knowing this spot got raided and we were beat. I had like 8 people in that IOP. U were not a dummy by any means. I was working there. I really don't know why u coming at me like that, like I forced ya to stay there or knew the spot was gonna get raided. I checked out your policy, but we only tried PHP, detox rez would be your best bet to make money after Jan 1ˢᵗ.*

DYLAN: *You threw me like two hundred bro, I got connects for two to three racks.*

BILL: *I didn't get paid on u the spot got raided bro that two hundred came out of my own pocket.*

DYLAN: *I ain't buyin that Bill, that shit got raided after I was there like like four months.*

BILL: *Early October that shit happened. Then we were gonna try to move ya and that didn't work out. But yah I didn't get paid after they raided the spot bro, I don't know why u think otherwise. I got burnt on a lot of people by her and so did other reps she fucked over at the time. I do five thousand on detox rez. So, I don't know who ur connects r now, but I thought you were gonna start working with me a while ago when u told me u were done being lazy and wanted to make some money. I work with doctor offices too man, so there's plenty of ways to get paid. I Just dunno why we are beating this dead horse aka Linda. Stiffing her reps after she got raided in October. R u hurting and in need of some bread?*

DYLAN: *I'm figuring out my next move. I wish we could work together but you can understand my lack of trust.*

I am grateful that Dylan ignored the frequent requests to delete text conversations. Dylan wanted it known, and this book to be written.

The longer he stayed, the larger the BONUS.

How much **BREAD** _do you think someone got for marketing my insurance?_

Sifting through each text helps explain how Dylan went from doing incredibly well in October to a bidding war in November. Other people contacted him for recovery programs when he was out between facilities. There were many other texts from people trying to get him, but nothing came of them. I believe much of what happened and what he witnessed while in the recovery centers aided in his demise.

With all this said, the hungry lurked, who coaxed and seduced him to take the bait, relapse, and cash in the chips. Here are the unedited text exchanges between them. I'll never know if Dylan would have made it had he remained at his sober house, without stress or referral agents taunting him. Would he be here today? Is there such a thing as a sober house with integrity?

Agent: Give him a call tonight.

Dylan: Appreciate you linkinup man, I got a lot of great people at my house but I needed a sponsor. I got a question.

AGENT: Shoot

DYLAN: How much bread do you think someone got for marketing my insurance for a few months PHP?

AGENT: Let me place u or at least run ur insurance so I can get before u run it with another shmuck. I m financially stable so I don't intend on keeping shit.

DYLAN: Yes this other kid is a shithead.

AGENT: I'll put u in the right hands so u can do business the right way directly after that but it depends on where u get placed cus some places need beds filled ASAP and will pay more

DYLAN: Threw me two hundred for sweating him but I'm annoyed.

AGENT: Yeah man, fuck that, I'll take care of you. Honestly around $1,200 to $ 2,200 I think every two weeks or less, send me ur policy I can verify those details and places that I know always pay me. But if u want me to investigate I can do that for u and have u still in Hollywood.

My boy actually just opened up a new halfway spot and he was the intake counselor at XXXXX a very reputable place and he's a solid ass dude, he'd be the direct line of connection so it would be all legit no middleman or extra people involved

DYLAN: *Different lOP or house?*

AGENT: *Depends*

AGENT: *He works his own spot but people still use whatever IOP they want*

DYLAN: *I dig my house n therapists I wish there was a shorter way to collect*

AGENT: *That's fine bro let me see what's going on.*

AGENT: *Hey Dylan, give me a shout I got a place set up for you with my friend.*

DYLAN: *I don't think I'm going to leave this place Man, I got really good people here.*

AGENT: *I will give you 2 grand to go and it should be around ten or fifteen days.*

DYLAN: *For PHP? (Partial hospitalization program)*

AGENT: *Yes, and u can still take Subs (suboxone)*

DYLAN: *I'm almost off subs*

AGENT: *U don't have to take subs, but it's an option, talk to my friend when he calls.*

DYLAN: *How can I do this?*

AGENT: *Ur in good hands brother, just trust the process my friend has paid me countless times.*

DYLAN: *Cool man I trust that, but I really don't want to leave my people, I'm really stuck.*

AGENT: *U won't have to but for a couple of weeks at most and then u can come back with a car and be set up. You won't get anywhere sticking in the same house with no money. Trust me, they want you broke so they can milk ur Insurance.*

DYLAN: *I got really good people in my life right now.*

AGENT: *And it is about to run out. I get that, but it's only temporary. it's not like your gonna have to turn ur phone in, or cut off contact from them. U simply*

I will

give you

two grand to

go and it should

be around

ten or

days.

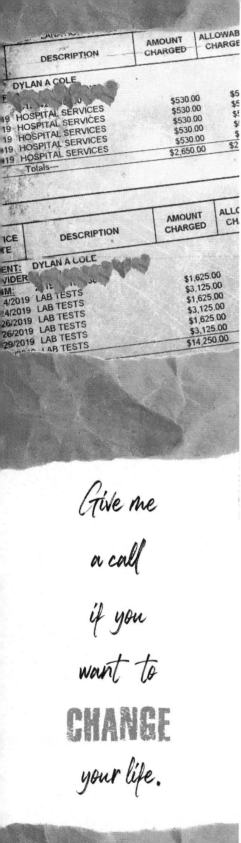

do PHP for a week or two. I send u money and ur insurance is good enough that they'll want to take u back.

AGENT: I have great news brother give me a call ASAP. OK cause this something I'm doing for you to put a couple grand in your pocket. I wouldn't steer u wrong like these fuck boys. And there's a greater deal on the table now for you.

DYLAN: Fuck man

AGENT: Just listen to me Dylan, pls.

DYLAN: I really don't want to leave this place.

AGENT: U can always come back.

AGENT: Give me a call if you want to change ur life I put in the work to get you in and paid two grand. That's a lot for me to do. After we get the money you can go back to ur old halfway, it's that simple,

DYLAN: I hear u

AGENT: I'm just tryin to help u get on ur feet. Give me a call If ur serious man, there's a lot of money making to be involved.

DYLAN: I'm in a house meeting, and yeah man, I hear you. I'm just trippin cuz I'm doing so well right now. I don't know if I wanna fuck with the way things are goin.

A few days passed between text messages when Dylan reached out to the Agent to ask if he knew of any doctors performing Naltrexone (FDA-approved drug that treats alcohol and opiate addiction) implants, which replace the oral or injected form lasting up to six months.

Years prior, I drove Dylan to a doctor for a Vivitrol injection which would have been good monthly, but he refused to go into the office. Seeing his text inquiry for Naltrexone spoke volumes about his sobriety dedication. I wish I had known; I would have arranged everything.

Would this have been his life's game-changer? Could it have increased his odds because, unlike Suboxone, it had to be surgically removed by a doctor? Watch the movie I suggested, *Body Brokers,* you'll learn about the scams associated with substance abusers, brokers, and the Naltrexone injection. I'm not adding a movie spoiler; watch the movie. Agent allegedly researched the implant, and the wheeling and dealing continued through November 2019.

By the first week of December 2019, again without notice, my son is on the street. It's that quick and simple. Somehow I missed the memo, including the one from my son. I'm in addiction year ten, and my kid's on the street. We had a Pink Cloud moment, I believed someone did hear my prayers, and then poof! The Goddamn lights went out! And the darkness sucked every ounce of hope from the pores of my soul. My son is not going to make it, is he? I can't stop the evil forces that surround him, can I?

A book aisle awaits me with literature explaining the consequences of life. It's sweetly written in a Verdana font, and printed on the finest, weighted paper. I assume Dylan was holding the ball, which he thought would hit a home run. He had it under control in his mind until suddenly, on the street with possessions in a garbage bag. He was no longer an insurance payout and refused to pay $ 2,000 a month in rent. Finally, he was vulnerable enough to accept Agent's proposal.

AGENT: *My friend is going to call you from a 908 number under the circumstances (due to Dylan being from NJ) don't talk to anyone else Dylan, please, I'm pulling strings for you. Don't accept help from no one else the human trafficking shit is real out there. People are bustin tail to get u in today.*

DYLAN: *I talked to your friend, seems like a good dude. And I trust you bro but cut me off right please. I got a kid and I'm going into a difficult life.*

AGENT: *Just don't talk about money to anyone else but me. That will fuck everything up.*

DYLAN: *Don't worry bro, let's split this shit right.*

AGENT: *I'm not worried about me I'm worried about u homies.*

Don't talk to anyone Dylan, **PLEASE,** I'm pulling strings for you.

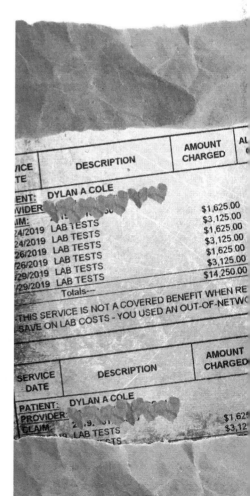

	DESCRIPTION	AMOUNT CHARGED	AL
ENT: DYLAN A COLE			
VIDER		$1,625.00	
IM:		$3,125.00	
24/2019 LAB TESTS		$1,625.00	
24/2019 LAB TESTS		$3,125.00	
26/2019 LAB TESTS		$1,625.00	
26/2019 LAB TESTS		$3,125.00	
29/2019 LAB TESTS		$14,250.00	
29/2019 LAB TESTS			
Totals---			

THIS SERVICE IS NOT A COVERED BENEFIT WHEN RE
SAVE ON LAB COSTS - YOU USED AN OUT-OF-NETWO

SERVICE DATE	DESCRIPTION	AMOUNT CHARGED
PATIENT: DYLAN A COLE		
PROVIDER		$1,62
CLAIM	LAB TESTS	$3,12

DYLAN: Oh yeah brother no worries I love it out here

AGENT: I got you man just sit tight and wait for John to conference you in with the coordinator. If they haven't already, they bout to. No doubt just got off the phone with him as soon as they get u in the door, I'll know around like what I'm lookin at for ur policy, hopefully they didn't rape ur policy too bad like I was saying they would. Put my name down as an emergency contact when U get there and say I'm ur sponsor and that my name is Jeremy or some shit, cause they monitor all their calls. So when ur in there don't call me about bread, but do u have a bank account I can send it to while you're out there? Stay the full thirty and they'll like u to stay at their PHP (partial hospitalization program).and It'll be a good example of a sober person tryna do right and they will love paying us for those type of people. Don't fuck around leave, break rules, or tell anyone what's goin on when ur in there OK please? It has gotten so strict out there now that's why John only wants u talking to me about shit like this cus we have a long business history, we know how to work it

DYLAN: We all set

AGENT: I got you trust, I been tryna tell u I would not steer u wrong.

DYLAN: I know, but I have some good family here, always will. But imma go make bread now that they left me no other choice. LoL

AGENT: Dylan please don't do anything stupid bro before going in seriously.

DYLAN: No man I'm going to drink a little and take some subs. Just enough to sell my story we're gonna be alright

AGENT: Call me when u can I need to go over things the sooner the better just so we're clear on everything beforehand. Use that number for me

as an emergency or my other one just in case for family. This is an emergency contact number text free app but delete our messages before u go in to cause I don't want anything possibly going wrong. I've had people search my phone and shit like some shady places and shit just gotta always be on point you're going to a good place

DYLAN: *OK, so that's contact for u?*

AGENT: *Yeah, but u can put both down say it's ur sponsor. That text free app should be good but write my other number down just in case, as like some other dude named James from Jersey or something*

DYLAN: *I'm sure this is all completely max degree lol, don't stress man*

AGENT: *Yeah bro we're legit as fuck lol. I just want everything for us to go easy and smooth sailing. U can work with John directly after this if u show him that u able to do this the right way.*

DYLAN: *They have my phone. I'm safe calling I 'Il hyu tomorrow.*

AGENT: *OK.*

After Dylan was admitted, the arranged N.J. sponsor contacted him. These referral agents are connected, coached, and financed by the pros. It's heart-wrenching to know that my son was a pawn. These bastards know that by baiting the ill, recovering substance abuser with money to relapse, they are a high risk for overdose and death. The deals will continue to be offered until the insurance benefits are cut off.

CHRIS: *Yo, it's your sponsor, you're safe there.*

DYLAN: *Is this all gonna work out well here?*

CHRIS: *Yeah*

DYLAN: *It's strict but I can be fine here*

CHRIS: *Insurance is most likely gonna take you off early if we try and move u out of there. I know it's strict but it will help. I was there before I knew. How it was, but when I left there my insurance cut-off afterwards. The longer the better my friend.*

Just don't talk about **MONEY** to anyone else.

DYLAN: *Are we gonna be straight or am I just sitting here. For no reason LOL it's super strict, calls are on speaker. $? Y $? N?*

CHRIS: *You'll be good bro, nowhere else will take your insurance, but they're working with you. Give me a call when ur free and not monitored.*

DYLAN: *Is it worth it tho?*

CHRIS: *And delete all texts*

DYLAN: *I will, are we getting paid or not?*

CHRIS: *Yes man cause there's nowhere else to go that will accept you.*

DYLAN: *OK, as long as I get paid, I'll deal with it.*

CHRIS: *Just don't talk about money to anyone else but me OK, that will OK everything up*

DYLAN: *Don't worry u gonna eat bro let's just split this shit right?*

I'll never know what materialized from Dylan's broker-based recovery center or if there was a payout. From the paperwork and texts, he was there from December 5 – 17, 2019. If he had received the money, he would have splurged and not reentered two more detox recovery centers.

After discharge, he was back on the street, and we put him in a motel from

December 18 through 21, 2019. He stayed at another referral agent's home from Dec 21 to 22 and was admitted into a new recovery center from December 23 to January 10, 2020.

I discovered a referral agent on Dylan's phone text who appeared to be a substance abuser connected to his sober house or affiliated with his IOP. Anthony began messaging Dylan in November 2019. Over the years, I've learned that these people change phones like a Kardashian changes outfits. Anthony knew some of the same people as Dylan. They knew which housemate escaped testing positive for substance abuse. Dylan did not use substances while in the program. I read text messages from other sober house roomies, asking for his urine to pass their test. While Dylan

DRUGS ALCOHOL

While Dylan waited for his next move to a new detox, he and Homie did drugs and alcohol.

RELAPSE

waited to be admitted into detox, he and Anthony did drugs and alcohol.

ANTHONY: I can swing by later so you can piss in a cup for me?

DYLAN: Yeah, I got u, just let me know what time so I'll drink water.

ANTHONY: WTF happened?

DYLAN: I was talkin shit on how corrupt Cali is and they didn't like it.

ANTHONY: What are you gonna do? Y u tryna go to treatment, it give u 2 stacks. (Two thousand)

DYLAN: I don't know if my insurance puts out still.

ANTHONY: What's ur info, I'll see wasup. Call me bro, wat u tryna do?

DYLAN: Scoop some up me n u.

ANTHONY: How many u want?

DYLAN: They 25? I def need 2-3 if you can spot a lil til tonight, Imma get some more.

ANTHONY: OK. How much money u got now? U down to kick it still or What? I wanna have a couple of drinks, I ain't gonna lie.

DYLAN: If you wanna front 15, I can double it in groceries.

Dylan requested some Jägermeister and Red Bull. Anthony was busy scoring some blues (oxys) for Dylan and trying to get him into another recovery center. Dylan got some methamphetamine on the street. He was resourceful, handed the homeless some of his possessions, played chess, and earned the meth. He was out of recovery for a few hours before relapsing. He had to be desperate for a buzz because he hated and avoided meth.

ANTHONY: Send me ur info bra.

DYLAN: For what rehab?

ANTHONY: Yes if u want if not fuck it.

DYLAN: Word yeah we can figure that shit out Later, I don't even know what my next move is yet.

ANTHONY: Yea U ain't tryna do it, u should not a said that bra, I hate liars.

DYLAN: Shit I don't know what I'm tryna do. I gotta go back in treatment soon we will make a move for some $. Hit me up today brotha if u wanna kick it. We can talk bout marketing my shit today too. I def need another blue today bro, I haven't slept.

Both Dylan and Anthony were plotting who to hit up next. A roommate at the sober house asked for tar (heroin). We paid for another night's motel room and provided money for what we had hoped was food. In the past, we gave gift cards but learned that, too, was pointless. There are many creative ways to barter for drugs, and groceries were one of them.

Dylan had $100 dollars, and Anthony smoked meth before meeting up with him. He offered Dylan some, who refused due to lost hours coming off Meth from the previous day.

What happens with substance abusers who find themselves confined to a sober house, IOP meetings, and at times, a feeling of house arrest; cravings will trump reasoning and consequence.

John, a sober house roomie, was looking for tar and woke up in a hospital a few weeks earlier. He lost his money and memory for about four hours. John had texted Dylan saying how much he hated himself, how stupid he was and how he feared not returning to the sober house. Luckily, he was returned to the same sober house after being discharged from detox. Dylan fully supported John's sobriety until he found himself kicked out and on the streets two weeks later. Here's a text exchange of Dylan encouraging John's sobriety:

JOHN: I don't know yet but worse comes to worse, I have one detox lined up, but I don't want to get the usual but sometimes only two if that so I don't know yet. I'll let you know.

DYLAN: Alright man, keep me posted. You can beat this shit man. It's just gonna ruin your life. I hope you bounce back.

JOHN: Yeah, I'm bouncing the fuck back yo fuck dis dumb Ass shit yo.

DYLAN: Well, you're alive, so there's still a chance.

JOHN: Yeah true, I still hate what I did on this run. I just can't believe I did what I did.

The reality and fragility of addiction, fast forward a couple of weeks after John was hospitalized, he's caved and is asking Dylan about tar. Dylan entertained John with his freedom, whereabouts, and evening plans.

DYLAN: I have no idea where to find it, I've been on Skid Row for six hours. Tell no one. LoL

JOHN: At the 7-11 by the center, LARC center. The guy in the car camping out front.

DYLAN: Shit, Craig's List Roofin Tar? LOL

JOHN: Yea bro I heard it's hard to find from a rando on Skid Row or Reddit. LOL

DYLAN: Start hittin anyone up

JOHN: I don't have anyone to hit up though I might be able to, but I don't know if I trust him. Should I try?

DYLAN: I would try and get a G, tell him we will take care of him.

JOHN: I think a G is eighty, but I'll ask. I would try the spot by the center if my boy doesn't answer.

DYLAN: I'm on Skidrow now, I'll be back that way soon.

JOHN: OK, I'd try to check it out there first cuz my boy is not answering. He said his boy with the tar isn't answering but he's getting pressed Blues, let me know if you want those. I think tar is better anyway.

DYLAN: OK, give me fifteen.

JOHN: I think they're thirty-five a pop. Yo, he said his boy with the black answered. My boy is George V from Miami, he said to hit him up about the tar.

DYLAN: Yo, I can get you a half a blue for twenty.

JOHN: Damn, no Tar? Fuck, I don't wanna OD cus I have no tolerance.

I've been on SKID ROW for six hours.

DYLAN: Do half a half.

JOHN: Tar lasts way longer.

DYLAN: Sniff and stay somewhere people will see you. Then if ur OK in an hour do a half, then do the other.

JOHN: I hate sniffing, fuck yo tar lasts way longer than that shit.

DYLAN: Yeah but I have no plugs yet.

JOHN: OK bro, yeah but do u or Dan have any rigs (needles)?

DYLAN: NO, you gotta sniff, I wouldn't wanna have u OD.

JOHN: Yes I'll do it, I would only, literally shoot a grain n a half. So it lasts longer. Fuck, I'll still do the half, the bigger half Is that cool? Fuck it, I don't care the bigger or whatever half. At this point let's wait till after the house meeting cuz it'll be easier for me to not get caught.

DYLAN: Cool

JOHN: I have someone you can hit up for just about anything. The guy delivers.

DYLAN: I'm thirty minutes from Hollywood.

JOHN: Damn, u r far as fuck. Try Craigslist and search for roofing materials. If there's no pic at all or a pic of a can, most importantly the phone number will be spelled out like 2one4sixnine, or something very close to that, or just roofing. The pic might have sheets of actual Roofing shit.

DYLAN: I can't find shit.

John provided Dylan with a number that he shared from his contact list. Contact's number was 0000000. That was the last of their text exchange. Lastly, I believe the following conversation was from a former sober house roommate. He knew Dylan and was on his way to California, possibly to the first sober house where Dylan had stayed. He also offered to make Dylan money for placement.

TY: Hope you are alright dude.

DYLAN: Kicked out of another joint. On to the next.

I can get you a half a BLUE for twenty,

Kicked out
of another

JOINT.

On to the next.

TY: Fuck that send me your info imma get you paid bro. I Just got 3 bandz in detox, and I got my phone.

DYLAN: I made it 14 days, but I got the boot. I can't do detox again. I'll bash my head in a wall.

TY: You don't have to do detox again man, I can send you to IOP and get you paid.

DYLAN: Thx baby girl where u at now.

TY: Palm Springs, it's fucking gorgeous out here bro. You wanna hit an IOP and get paid though I can make it happen.

DYLAN: That sounds like the wave bud.

TY: Hit me with your insurance info dig, I'll get you in tonight, Sub (suboxone) maintenance also an option.

DYLAN: I just got off subs. LoL

TY: I'm just tryna get you in my dude. I don't want you out on the street. Especially if I can do something about it and you can be next to me and get paid. Alright buddy, You're going to Malibu, you're going to get a call, you know the routine, tell them you're sick blah blah blah and just make sure you be ready to go tomorrow and the biggest thing is we cannot get paid if you ama so please don't. LoL

DYLAN: I won't lol, I'll shut my mouth round therapist too.

TY: Thank you kind sir let me know when they call you.

DYLAN: I have all these bitches hitting me up, the one place wants to take my phone and shit.

TY: Which one?

DYLAN: But are they paying 2 racks.

TY: Yeah, they pay 2 racks tho tats the catch for no phone.

DYLAN: I'm down, I guess. How long?

TY: That's true help right?

DYLAN: Lol, yea, I don't care those places spoil u, I just hate not having my sheet.

TY: *And 14 days for 2 racks if you do more you'll get more tho, 2 will get you 3.*

DYLAN: *They are doin Italian on xmas. I can do 21 if you're gonna pay me out 100% bro. If u don't, I'm gonna post our texts and then run naked into San Francisco traffic.*

TY: *I will dog, I'm not gunna burn you.*

The text exchange ended with Ty ignoring a few of Dylan's messages, and there wasn't evidence of the promised payout for Dylan's relapse and admission to detox.

Dylan spent eight out of twelve months in recovery centers, all but one through a referral agent. When he decided to return home, he was angry, agitated, and still not sober. He promised to abstain from heroin but would drink alcohol and said, in a twisted way, we should be grateful.

When we suggested a men's sober house, the lies and manipulation began. Dylan beat us down through phone calls, texts and threatened suicide. He sent his father a video of his hand filled with pills saying, "My phone battery is 10%. Bye, Dad, I love you." I had earlier in the month blocked Dylan's phone after he verbally abused me for not sending money.

Days evolve with no news is good news, and no matter how tainted we are, not an hour goes by without worry's painful imagery. Parental scar tissue is not impervious to a restless night with clenched fists. From what I later would interpret from Dylan's text messages, he took too many prescribed meds, and returned to the last detox for a roof over his head.

Yeah,

they pay

2 RACKS.

He nourished Mr. Hyde, and seldom switched to Dr. Jeckyll. Being sober brought him physical and emotional pain. It had to be silenced, leaving no room for kindness and love.

Homecoming

By January 2020, Dylan's life had spiraled into uncertainty and betrayal. At the time, we had no idea he was being trafficked and blending prescribed meds with other substances for relapse purposes. Even the healthiest physiology would be in danger, never mind a substance abuser, whose body profoundly challenges its life force.

We tried every means to alter the story, but we were not the author. Dylan held the pen, and we were his characters. When he decided it was time to come home, there would be no stopping him. Knowing the odds, we refused to send him a plane ticket. He began working with his friends for money who were oblivious to the agony of having their child, 25, heroin-addicted, and about to die — a segment in life they were yet to live and hopefully never would.

As expected, none of his friends came through. Had Dylan made money from relapsing, there would have been evidence in his text messages and a massive spending spree. Eventually, Dylan's father caved and sent him an airline ticket. There was so much toxicity between us that I couldn't see the light at the end of the tunnel. The horror movie would soon loop.

Two years prior, I had put life on hold by closing my business, boarding the Arizona house, and forgoing our Airbnb. I'm not portraying a victim but sharing life's reality. It's what a parent who loves their child more than life itself will do. For several years, I endured Dylan's toxic verbal abuse. It wasn't my son calling me, "Fucking cunt, bitch, loser of a mother." His inner suffering, heroin,

Dylan had the PEN, and we were his characters.

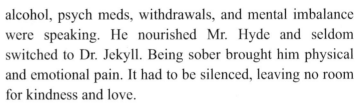

alcohol, psych meds, withdrawals, and mental imbalance were speaking. He nourished Mr. Hyde and seldom switched to Dr. Jekyll. Being sober brought him physical and emotional pain. It had to be silenced, leaving no room for kindness and love.

We needed to find Dylan a sober home, which he was not thrilled about, and I thought I'd diffuse some of the tension by briefly returning to Arizona when he returned.

Dylan had missed his flight with hours to kill before the next. We hadn't spoken in a couple of weeks, but I broke the ice when I transferred cash to his debit card. He was surprised to see my message and signature purple heart and asked, "Why?" Joking, I responded, "In case the plane crashes." We shared some dark humor and touched on the rumors of the new virus called Covid. He was excited to return home, make peace with me, and pick up where he had left off with his son. In a month, life on earth would collapse from a pandemic. In retrospect, the lockdown would have forced Dylan to return home.

In preparation for his arrival, we got his car road-ready and a bond from his grandmother's estate available to cash. While he transitioned back into society, we would help subsidize his rent, and anything else he needed. We had hoped that his three-year-old son, who he missed terribly, would be the catalyst for his sobriety. My husband, his girlfriend Jackie, and I, never understood how mental illness, addiction, and trauma go together. Dylan arrived home on January 28; his 26th birthday was February 2; he was pronounced deceased on February 6, 2020.

Within the first year of leaving a treatment program, a substance abuser has an 85 percent chance of relapse. I often guilt myself for having been so naive about brain chemistry. To those struggling with a child's addiction and the verbal abuse they can inflict, know it's not your child speaking. I have a solid reputation for being patient, which Dylan repeatedly tested. I couldn't force him to stop taking prescription meds or heroin. Nor could I convince him to

pursue trauma therapy. In the end, he was unnecessarily destroyed by each.

When we see wounded people labeled mentally ill in the streets or our homes, we don't understand their struggle. I often dwell on what happened to my son before his death. I know the prescribed meds were a nightmare, causing more harm than good. Perhaps they work for some people, but for many substance abusers, they're dangerous.

Was Dylan born chemically imbalanced, with a genetic destiny predisposed to addiction? Some experts believe this to be true, and other experts don't. There was an increased chemical imbalance due to his substance abuse. Were his ever-changing prescribed meds the tip of the iceberg?

A couple of weeks after Dylan passed, I received a text from him through iCloud Messenger. I never received messages that way; it was haunting and written on February 9, 2019, almost a year prior to the exact day of death. At first, I thought it was a postdated suicide note. It explains in a poetic voice his anguish and how he battled addiction. I felt a brief encounter with comfort, feeling that he reached out after death.

February 9. 2019

Dope

Started with Percocet, I wish I could take it back. I was failing in high school, always onto harder drugs, friends ask me why fool?

But I couldn't help it, I wanted to have fun before I turned numb and selfish.

I was a teen selling pills and weed. Things didn't change up until I had an addiction to feed.

I was with some friends chilling playing cards, we had a bunch of coke sniffing and kicked it in the yard.

We were all geeked up and I knew sleeping was going to be hard.

I wanted to come down and just try to relax, that's when my homie threw a stamp in my lap.

He said, "It's up to you, it will help bring you down" so I snorted that shit and just laid on the ground.

I laughed and felt amazing, such a different high, if only I knew how self-destructive it would be to my life.

I started out snorting, never caught a habit, I knew it would sell so I always fucking had it.

A young wild kid who just wanted to party and make money. So, I'd hang with girls and sell 100$ Bunnys.

The suburban hustle was crazy filled with profit, but it wasn't fucking worth it, I wish I could have saw it.

It only took a day that changed my world, all in the hands of an addicted young girl.

We would make sales cruising in my car, one thing led to another and she stuck that needle in my arm.

That was it, it was all over. That warm euphoric rush, I'll never be sober.

I fell in love with the greatest feeling. I was hooked, pawning and stealing.

My greatest regret, I broke so many hearts. The ones I loved most left with ptsd and scars.

They don't understand, I can't fucking stop. Even after six ODs I'm not afraid to drop.

I'm suicidal and depressed, I just want to numb. A struggling soul and now I have a son.

I beg for the day it will end; it needs to come.

Damian needs me, I can't OD or press the cold steel to my temple from the barrel of a gun.

This is a war within my mind that needs to be won.

I fight for my son, I fight for myself, I fight for his mom. I'll beat it one day I refuse to be a pawn.

I love my girl, and a queen deserves a king, I want to be alive for what the future will bring.

She thinks I'm worth it, tells me to kick this shit that I fuckin deserve it.

I can't leave my son in this cold world alone. He needs a family, and he needs a home.

I need to not feel so empty and know I'm not alone. If my son ever feels this broken,

I'll never let him face this on his own.

Years earlier, I had found the girl who plunged the first needle into Dylan's vein. He was 19 and had left a social media app open on his computer. With full barrels, I attacked her. I don't recall everything about the conversation, but she did a great job of self-defense and explained far more than I could comprehend. We talked about heroin's demonic force and the call to be numbed. She had been through her share of detox, rehabs, and had a story to match my son's. She was intelligent, with hopes, wishes, and dreams. Her passion was horses, and I was a horse owner. As we spoke, my heart softened. It appeared this would be a recurring theme for the rest of my life. My initial anger would turn inward and become kinder energy.

I started this book 19 months after my son's death. Grief is still sinking in and out of my heart. My son had overdosed nine times that I knew of, and according to his text messages, probably more like 13. I was in Arizona when I received my husband's frantic call, saying, "I think he's gone." On autopilot, I began instructing him where to find and how to use Narcan (a medicine that reverses the effects of an opioid overdose). I quickly paced while waiting for my husband's response, as we weren't amateurs to overdose but had created a false sense of security.

For the most part, Dylan looked dead each time he overdosed, but he always woke up. Of course, my husband

I hung up the phone, and SCREAMED for hours.

was shocked; he had never participated alone and missed some of Dylan's worst moments. This time, he would be the only one to absorb the unimaginable. He was frightened and fumbling with the Narcan, and I asked, "Have you called 911?" Distraught, he answered, "No." I told him to hang up and call.

My denial owned the moment, and I felt the meaning of time standing still. My increased saliva and constant swallowing soured my stomach. Why wasn't my husband calling back to say that Dylan was going to the ER? There was a definitive mental block protecting me from considering the truth. The pressure in my chest longed for answers. I ended the wait and called back.

There was a lot of background noise when my husband answered, and he put me on speaker. I asked what was happening, and he responded, "The EMTs, police, and detectives are here. He's gone." Yanked through the veil of death, I, too, ceased to be but continued breathing. Each letter H-E-S G-O-N-E branded my heart like the sear of a hot iron. Catatonic blurts slithered from my tongue. "I don't want him touched, NO autopsy, we know why he died." Last, I asked if there was a syringe. Only an empty glassine was found, which meant he snorted the fatal dose. Dylan always said that if he ever touched heroin again, it would be to kill himself.

I hung up the phone, stepped away from consciousness, and screamed for hours: blood-curdling screams, a total loss of control and awareness. I had left my body and watched this person marching room to room, screaming.

On a good day, the airport was four hours roundtrip. I booked a plane, and while waiting for the driver, my body went into shock, I couldn't stop shivering. When I arrived at the airport, my wallet was missing. It must have fallen out of my pocket while I was shivering. I returned home finding it on the couch and booked a red-eye flight that evening.

My husband met me at the airport; our ride home remained silent. My son had died in his bed, in my grandson's room. Despite the hundreds of times, I envisioned his death, I am grateful that his life ended in his home. My heart breaks for my husband, who must live with the final vision of finding his son deceased and watching his body taken out in a bag.

The fog of grief is intense, and we move through it somewhat unconscious. I went directly to the bed, where Dylan took his last breath. I grasped the pillows and sheets, searching for any part of him. The physical was gone, and I needed something of him to hold and feel. My body folded over, cradling his hoodie and hat, snorting the fabric as he did heroin. I squeezed its hollowness, begging for his scent.

I was so damn angry at him. All the years spent fighting his demons, and we lost! Along with eternal tears was a flood of rage. I don't like the word "dead." The term has a stabbing force, an underlying power that disarms my ability to function. He's passed, left us, gone, is how I fill in the blanks. It's a struggle during the early grief until we accept that all of us will die; in life, nothing is permanent. Dylan's phone texts revealed how it all went down. The notorious Paterson, NJ, was where Dylan typically picked up heroin and pills. A female he knew mutually through her boyfriend (who had overdosed and died two months prior) delivered Dylan his fatal dose. The only other place Dylan visited was a friend's house when he first arrived home, where I believe he received the other drugs in his system. I needed to fill in the blanks because the urine analysis showed amphetamine, heroin, Xanax, cocaine, Fentanyl, and opiates.

Both my husband and I suffered immense guilt from our son's passing. Our words were meant to save, not destroy. We came from a ten-year battle, war-torn souls with an exhausted arsenal. Initially, we believed the pressures of getting him into a sober home had pushed him over the final edge. He was also furious we did not allow alcohol in the house. It was the first time we put our foot down on solid ground. It had to stop. I texted him that no

All the years spent fighting his DEMONS and we lost!

Even if
it remained ugly,
we were still
HOPEFUL

parent deserves this life or should walk in these shoes. He answered, "okay," and the next day, he ordered heroin.

He never answered another text I sent about coming to Arizona for a couple of weeks. We had been through years of these pitfalls, and nothing ever changed. Even if it remained ugly, we were still hopeful.

Another massive trigger for Dylan was the absence of his friends on his birthday. He was painfully disappointed none tried to see him after eight months away. They moved on with their lives. I believe that wounded him significantly. He found a stored bottle of champagne in the basement and turned to his Xbox friends to celebrate his birthday. His mother "ghosted" him, he had arguments with Jackie and his father—another perfect storm.

After a visit with his son, he called a dealer in Paterson for Xanax and blues (Oxycodone). After eight months of addiction recovery, the demons who never left his side tapped his shoulder once again. A decade of rehab, clinics, therapists, psych wards, IOP meetings, outpatient, ERs, doctors, and numerous prescriptions could not save him.

The last text I sent Dylan was an invite to see Russell Brand's *Recovery Tour,* which was coming to New York City. While Dylan was in rehab, I had forwarded Russell's books, and he liked him. It was a matter of a few hours before taking his last breath. He answered "yes" to the tour.

That's how it goes, and I'm sure you've seen people post pictures of their loved ones smiling hours before taking their own life. We have no idea when facing the last moment with a loved one, and there's no escape from the painful realities of being human.

At first, I felt Dylan had died by suicide. For many years, he had threatened that he would kill himself. I feared finding him hanged or shot in the head and had personally known family and others who died by suicide. Dylan posted suicidal memes on social media, convincing us he'd carry it out one day. Those images haunted those who loved him. But he had a son; would he have killed himself?

He knew the odds were against him; a broken spirit pulled the trigger, with Fentanyl in the chamber. In the end, it was not the comforting blanket of numbness from heroin, but to end for a moment, or forever, the pain he carried in his tortured heart and soul.

"Nanny, look what I found."

HE WAS VULNERABLE

ACCIDENT OVERDOSE

12
The Law

My grandson's room had the bed where his father took his last breath. Before his next visit, I had searched every inch of the space. Within a couple of days, I gave the green light.

I was folding towels in the bathroom when my grandson said, "Nanny, look what I found." I glanced and dropped to my knees. His little hands held a bundle of heroin tied by a rubber band and stamped *New Arrival*. Had he opened, smelled, or tasted the powder, he would have died.

There are no words to measure my gratitude for my grandson's awareness. I asked where he found the packets, and he brought me to the windowsill in his room, pointing to a toy car.

Without question, Dylan loved his son with all his heart. I realized his death was not suicide but an *accidental* overdose. Placing heroin in his son's toy car meant he intended to live, not die. Purchasing a bundle said he was planning on using it again.

Dylan's last month of life ironically included coaching the gal who delivered the heroin to go into a treatment program. He was known for his supportive friendship, care of others, and encouraging sobriety and strength. His heart was in the right place when he returned home. But he was vulnerable, and the girl who delivered heroin made it convenient for him.

Dylan's case detective told me to bring the heroin and pills to the state police station. I placed everything into a baggie and drove to the nearest one. The building was small with little signage. I entered a narrow lobby that guided me to a two-way mirror. I assumed my position by

His
LITTLE
HANDS
were
holding
a bundle of
HEROIN.

The

NARCOTICS

department was

overloaded

the mirror and waited for seconds that felt like minutes. A male voice asked what my purpose was, and the first thing spewed from my mouth, "I'm dropping off my son's heroin." I was nervous, and it only got worse when the frustrated trooper emerged from the door. Doing his job, he began by asking me who, what, when, and where questions, which inevitably made me feel dirty. I mentioned my case detective's name, and he said I was in the wrong county. I didn't know; I had driven to the nearest one.

Scared and innocent, I handled the heroin and pills too loosely for the officer's liking. A baggie of Fentanyl-laced heroin was the last thing he wanted to deal with that morning. Even airborne, Fentanyl can kill if inhaled.

I got back into the car and drove to my county's state police station. As soon as I entered the building, a young trooper greeted me. When I told him what I was holding, he looked perplexed and said he would return with a detective, but before leaving, he handed me a statement form. He instructed me, for the record, to write my heroin tale. With Dylan gone less than two weeks, his death remained surreal. I was in a state of shock that transported numbness through my bloodstream. I had to write who murdered him, and her name was Fentanyl. Moments like these would echo forever, and I'd have to inhale and hold. Had I not wanted the heroin analyzed, I would have flushed it down the toilet to avoid reliving the trauma.

Slowly the door opened, and out walked a veteran detective. He sat next to me, and I felt reassured, not interrogated. We spoke at length, and he explained much of what hadn't been mentioned by the detective on my son's case. His gentle conversation steered from years of knocking on parent's doors to deliver the sad news.

The narcotics department was overloaded by the Fentanyl and Covid-19 pandemic. Anxious for justice, I had the evidence: glassines, pills, and information on the dealer. I exposed my innocence by not touching the baggie's contents. I asked the detective how long I'd wait for the results. His answer: "Over a year."

LAST CALL

His heart was in the right place
when he returned home.

My red flags

flashed

FURIOUSLY.

I learned about the laws for prosecuting dealers of Fentanyl-laced narcotics. One significant fact was the deceased's blood, and urine could not contain any additional drugs or alcohol. If the deceased also had evidence of marijuana or beer, the dealer could not be prosecuted. It's INSANE!

It had taken only one day to receive a urine toxicology result from the county morgue. Dylan's analysis contained amphetamine, cocaine, Xanax, heroin, opiates, and Fentanyl. I looked into the eyes of the detective, asking, "Then why the hell am I doing this if we already know the urine result?"

Was there such a thing as heroin laced with the drugs found in Dylan's urine? No, said the detective. The drugs in Dylan's urine were too expensive to cut into heroin, and my answer was right there. Why without a case, were detectives holding my son's possessions for a month. Wasting time analyzing the heroin bundle was pointless unless there was a hidden agenda unbeknownst to me.

I had been pulling together a caseload without a case and foolishly updating the detective. I wanted Dylan's phone hacked and offered to pay the department whatever it cost. But they would not hack or release it until the case was closed. I thought, what case? Was it due to the Covid outbreak or business as usual?

Before Dylan's death, my husband had seen him talking to a female sitting in a brown SUV in the driveway. More intriguing, the morning Dylan passed, an unknown female direct-messaged my husband on Facebook asking how Dylan was doing. Who would contact a parent they didn't know to check on a friend? Also odd was that Dylan's passing was not yet public at the time. My red flags lashed furiously, convinced she was the dealer, probably suffering from guilt. I was so damn vigilant, trying to retrace each of Dylan's steps after he arrived home from California.

Once Dylan's passing was posted on Facebook, our female contact became chattier and reached out for my cellphone number. I searched her social-media accounts and found a picture of her in front of a brown SUV. This female knew who sold Dylan the heroin. She was working with her town's detective and planning to set the dealer up for an arrest. I flipped when she asked to see Dylan's death certificate. Was she looking for the cause of death and whether she'd be implicated? I told my case detective, who replied, "It's out of our jurisdiction." It would be up to me to find answers.

I called, leaving a message with the detective connected to this female informant. It was the early days of the Covid shutdown, and not about Dylan. I waited a couple of weeks before hearing back from him. But it was worth the wait. The detective was warm and friendly and had known Dylan for years previously when we lived in the same town. He assured me that the female informant was not the dealer but someone with connections to the drug community who wanted to help.

I had no experience with the law other than what Dylan had brought to the table over the years. All I knew about police work I learned from the detective shows of my youth. We were in court a couple of times for traffic violations and underage matters, where I had hired a defense attorney to protect Dylan's reputation and record. My son's case became my murder mystery. I wanted to know who killed him, yet knew that when he had ordered the heroin, he killed himself. Asking the detectives if the evidence was fingerprinted must have made excellent breakroom laughter.

Each day I dug deeper in search of clues and connections. Waiting over thirty days for the detective to return Dylan's phone felt like an eternity. Thanks to Covid, the detective on my case wasn't working regular office hours and didn't check email from home. The world was in chaos. Social media pounded us with deserted streets, cities, schools, ventilator shortages, global victim death counts, and empty supermarket shelves.

I only wanted confirmation from the detective when I could retrieve my son's possessions. That was all that was

It would be up to me to find ANSWERS.

ADDICT ADDICTION

Doesn't have to be a maze.

Doesn't have to

JERSEY STATE

BAG

OF BA

BADGE NUMBER

#

Page 1 of 1

NEW JERSEY STAT

DATE OF IMPOUND

CASE NUMBER

ITEM NUMBER(S) IN BAG

BAG/ARTICLE # OF BAGS/

TO REMOVE CONTENTS

20-I1-00

Desc: [PHONE] App

Sussex County Pros

important, and it's what I thought about each waking hour. It completely distracted me from Covid madness. Grief had thrust me into a fearless whirl. On day 34, the case detective informed me that Dylan's possessions would be released, adding a time and location to meet.

My husband and I walked into the dank waiting room of the courthouse. From behind the safety glass, a clerk looked up, smiled, and asked who we were meeting. After saying the detective's name, I eagerly awaited the door's buzz, and to be guided through the office. When faced with the reality of my unreasonable expectations, my emotions swelled.

It's hard to express what that moment felt like, I was frightened yet full of joy when I received my son's possessions. I was finally bringing him home. The buzzer never opened the detective's door, but instead, the front door swung open, adding a winter blast our way. A male officer holding two blue papers called out my name. Thirty-four days of holding my breath, and that's how it went down. Begging like a dog, hoping to be noticed and thrown a bone. The wait was over. The officer grunted, "Sign here," and handed me two crackling plastic bags with Dylan's phone and iPad. Thankfully the grief fog was thick, and I was numb. After digesting the experience, I composed a letter to the case detective.

To: Detective Jones
Mon, Mar 16, 2020, at 6.53 am

It's been a couple of days since I received custody of Dylan's possessions. I'm assuming that this is my cue, the case is closed. I wasn't anticipating a sit-down conference with either detective. I was, however, expecting more than standing in a dank lobby and being handed two blue custody receipt papers to sign. A lobby that matched the scenario perfectly and Detective Smith's lack of humane communication skills. Just a day in the life of a detective, weekly OD case, and druggie off the streets.

I only wanted confirmation from the detective when I could retrieve my son's

POSSESSIONS

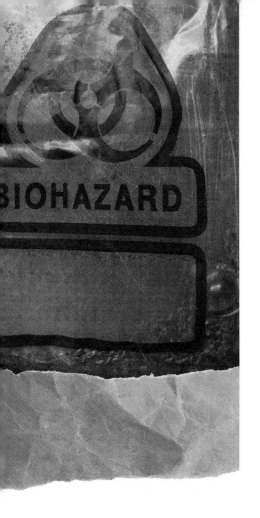

A constant pinball being flipped from one GUILT to another.

Previously, I had discussed with you that I didn't expect compassion due to Dylan's history of drug use. I mentioned that you're probably busy with numerous like cases. In so many words, you said that you 'did care' about each case, my case, and that's why you took the job you did.

I'm forever grateful to (our former hometown) Detective Ciccone. While remaining professional in his position and speaking from the heart, he explained the laws with heroin, distribution, criminal charges, and Dylan's situation. I have no words to express how comforting and important that was for me the two weeks following my son's death. The immediate results from the urine test detected other drugs in his system. When I handed over the heroin and oxys to the (county) State Trooper, he also explained the laws. Since the case was in your hands, I must ask, will I be informed of the bloodwork, heroin, and oxy pill results? Will there be a written, case-closed letter?

No matter what the history is of substance abuser, they were once a beautiful child, brother, husband, father, and human being. And as survivors of their death, we all share similar fear, guilt, rehab history, and enabling. When the death from an overdose finally takes our loved one, and in my case, a child away; we are destroyed for life. Grief struck with a heart that HURTS from crying and not being able to breathe correctly. Our brains, a constant pinball being flipped from one guilt to another, to what if's and should have been. We are lost with a history of years of hope while envisioning a happy ending to the madness. And for many, we endured some of the ugliest visions humanly possible.

Why did I bother writing this email? I've documented a decade's worth of life with Dylan's addiction. Experiences in multiple ERs, CPRs, fights with doctors, rehabs, looney bins over-medicating him. Suboxone, Methadone, Mexico, and Ibogaine.

Profiteering rehabs encourage relapse for referral fees, criminal charges, and insurance fraud. Happy Oaks & St. Christopher's Behavioral dumping substance abusers on the street with multiple psych meds. During these encounters, all I wished for was that a kind, motherly type nurse be on duty. One who would get me through the 'he's over 18' no tell rules.

Detective Jones, in my case, and most likely in so many others, we've been pulled through life's ringer. So, all I'm suggesting is when the time comes to hand over a loved one's objects, give them a compassionate moment and explain what to expect or not expect for closure. They'll be suffering for the rest of their lives, as they did long before you acquired their loved one's possessions.

Laura Cole

The detective did respond with emails and texts, trying to make good of a bad situation, but in my heart, it was too late. No attempt of sincerity would work, and I let the detective know my feelings. There's an immense lack of grief education among civil servants and medical professionals. The very people engaged with the grief-stricken don't receive the necessary training. We've accepted such behavior, but it's wrong. I learned there is also a lack of grief training and expertise in psychology.

Each of us experiences life differently, and perhaps I was expecting too much when the world was in chaos. I don't know if it would have been handled differently pre-Covid, but I hope my letter encourages the detective in the future to share kindness when handing over the possessions of a deceased child.

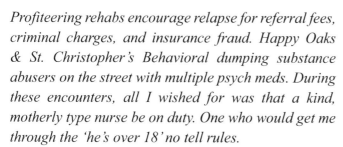

They'll be suffering for the rest of their lives, as they did long before you acquired their LOVED ONE'S possessions.

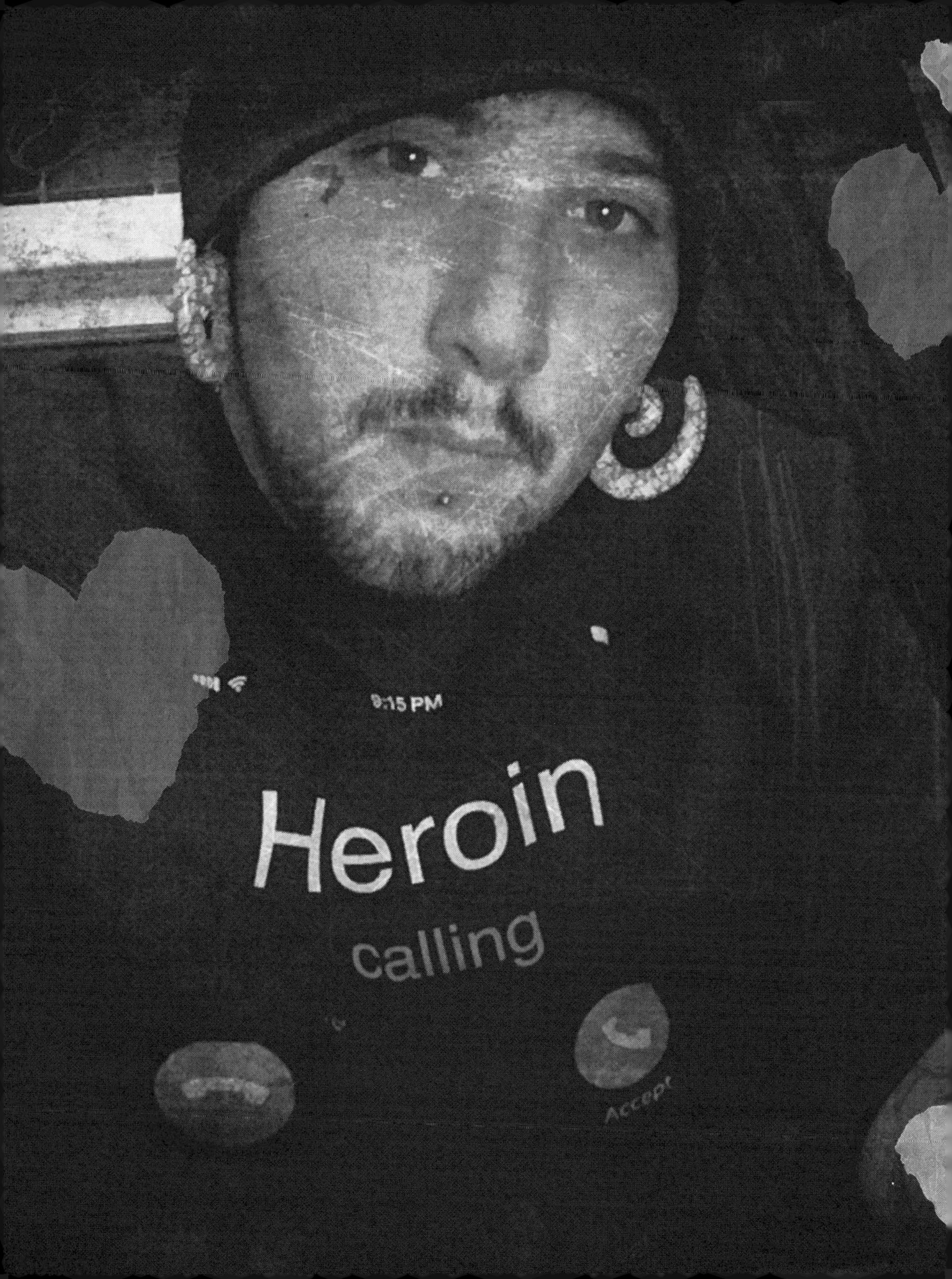
Heroin
calling
Accept

13

I Believe in Miracles

The detective on our case let me down, but a month's worth of waiting was over. We drove home with Dylan's possessions tightly wrapped in plastic, sitting on my lap. The bag's contents, Dylan's name, and death date were scribbled in black marker. A barcode sticker with the state police's county sealed the top.

The moment was surreal; months later, I realized the gift of grief fog. Our brains are incredible and find a way to protect our hearts. I didn't have a last vision, body, or coffin. Dylan's cell phone became the physical body that I was missing.

I charged the phone and searched online for a cellphone hacker when I returned home. Apple gives us three strikes with a passcode; I couldn't chance to guess. Jackie suggested using my husband's passcode, which I found odd. In my bedroom, illuminated only by a laptop, I held Dylan's phone and keyed in the passcode. The screen shifted and opened the phone. My chest caved, and both Jackie's and my eyes blurred from disbelief. Finally, the truth would be revealed.

If your loved one dies, before the body is removed, try face or fingerprint recognition to open their phone. It provides an opportunity to change passwords. I say this not to invade private space but to gain priceless photos, memories, and in my situation, evidence, and closure. If I didn't respect my son's privacy, I'd undoubtedly hear his scolds from the ethereal. I needed to know why, why he ordered heroin. How did it all go down, his last day's moments?

I needed to know WHY.

My need
to process his
DEATH
overrode everything.

From my son's phone, I'd also assemble a compilation of precious photos, videos, jokes, and texts to put into a journal for his son to enjoy someday. He would know his father's humor, thoughts, music taste, voice, and laughter.

My son, my baby of 26 years, was gone. I needed to understand Dylan's psyche, rehab stressors, drugs, and dealers during his last months. I would suffer the rest of my days and needed answers as to why he chose to use heroin that day. While writing this book, I typed, cried, and blew my nose a thousand times. I was never sure which sentence would slam my face into the sand. Sometimes, it's a given, and sometimes it's not. But no one has a right to judge my motherhood and choices.

Holding my son's life story on his phone challenged my integrity, yet my need to process his death overrode everything. Immediately, I found the texts and the girl who dealt the fatal dose. Once I had a name, I turned on Dylan's Facebook and searched his friend list. Within a few seconds of locating her page, her Facebook's active light turned off. She realized Dylan's phone was unlocked and quickly unfriended him.

A wonderful childhood friend of Dylan's kept in contact with my husband and me. She is equipped with Mother Teresa's empathy and carries a hospice nurse's title. When Facebook failed, she bestowed another gift by providing me with the dealer's phone number. She knew a friend of a friend. I'm forever indebted to her support during the most crucial times, and still, today, she reigns a beam in my foundation.

I needed to read every text between the female and Dylan. I learned that she was the former girlfriend of Sam, an acquaintance of Dylan's, who had overdosed and died in December 2019. Dylan's condolences on Sam's FB page were haunting. In less than two months, he, too, would be gone. In his text to Dylan, Sam describes his battle with heroin. Dylan suggested Sam get into a treatment center.

Dylan: It's a solid rehab I think, just tell them u can't be in Jersey.

Sam: Yeah man, I need to get out of here if I want any chance of getting clean. Tried to just do IOP but when I'm not getting high, that's all I think about and it feels like life's so boring without it. LOL Fucking addiction man, is the hardest shit I've ever been through in my life so far. So used to that lifestyle, it's all I know honestly, and just the thought of changing that scares me, it's fucked up.

I'll call her Sophie, and I don't consider her the dealer, only Dylan's delivery driver. They began exchanging texts after Sam's death in late December. Dylan had done quite a bit of coaching, along with treatment-center suggestions. Sophie, covered by Medicaid, had attended a brief treatment with a local hospital and had been discharged early due to fighting with another patient. She told Dylan she would schedule another appointment and hopefully be readmitted. She was tired of the heroin trek into the hood, being dopesick, and feared getting pulled over. She had a series of traffic violations and a court warrant. Like most in her position, Sophie was tired of life. She was snorting too much Fentanyl-laced heroin, which landed her face down over the porcelain bowl.

Dylan began joking with Sophie about his plans when returning home. He said no to heroin but would drink with his friends. He was revving up for party time with no mention of drugs. Sophie continued her heroin purge, suboxone, dope sickness, and the need to pick up heroin. After she scored a few bags, she shared how "Grooovvvy" she was feeling. The day before Dylan's return to NJ, he and Sophie shared a misery text.

January 27th

Sophie: I'm tired of being sad, I'm a happy person. Even if the happiness is fake, I hate misery. Not my lifestyle.

His dad said he heard a GURGLING snoring noise.

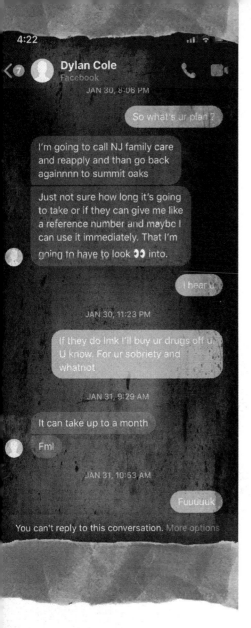

I'll buy ur **DRUGS** *off you.*

Dylan: I hear u. I'm the opposite. Always miserable and faking it. I love to distract or make music to lessen the load.

Sophie: Aww

Dylan: My life sucks. LOL

Sophie: I'm pretty sure the bags I get from Paterson have fent in them. You're saying if I snort too many I can OD?

Dylan: Oh, for sure! Just start small, a bag or two. Wait a while before you use again.

Sophie: Like today, I already did like seven and I'm puking face. Not trying to be gross like I'm torn up. Feeling grooovvyy. Actually a 9.

Dylan: LMAO, don't overdo it boo. I'm jelly (jealous)

Sophie: I won't, and don't be, I should be getting clean right now, super pissed about my insurance.

Dylan: I gotta do the opposite, lose this sober weight n then get clean with no meds. Let's switch, I'll take buns. LMAO

Sophie: I'm worried about gaining weight. I swear, I'll starve myself.

Dylan: Just don't take a fuckload of pills. They will try putting u on them.

Sophie: I won't.

Dylan arrived safely in NJ, and Sophie texted him to say she was at the hospital and hoped to enter treatment. In the meantime, she scored more heroin. That's what many substance abusers do before entering detox, one last hurrah. Dylan asked her how many "buns" or bricks she picked up. He suggested if her tolerance was low, not to do too much. Sophie added, "Yeah, I know my problem is when I have them, I do them, but I only snort." Dylan responded that she had less chance of overdosing, but Fentanyl was still dangerous.

Sophie ran into a few snags with insurance, with treatment delayed. As I read their text exchange, I realized this was where Dylan's intentions had shifted, and he could

The image on the left shows an iMessage conversation:

no longer ignore an opportunity to obtain some bags of heroin.

Dylan: *If they do let me know. I'll buy ur drugs off u. U know, for sobriety and what not.*
Sophie: *It can take up to a month.*
Dylan: *Fuuuuuk.*

The next couple of days were heavy. Dylan was angry with all of us who cared and loved him the most. We were pushing for him to go to a sober living home. His relationship with his father, Jackie, and me was toxic. Combine that with us not allowing alcohol in the house, created the fuel to ignite him. His birthday came and went without celebration. His friends moved on with their lives and hadn't gone out of their way to see him. He must have been feeling lost, and lonely. Certainly, defeated because his addiction had only been medicated, and its root cause neglected.

By February 3, he was looking to use. He texted Sophie, asking if she knew of anyone heading to Paterson. He told her, "Shit just bad here with my family. Been looking for Xanax."

Sophie gave him directions to a gas station corner that always supplies Xanax. She told him when her warrant and tickets were cleared, she would take him, but wouldn't let him get dope, laughing after the text. Dylan said he'd probably be going himself. It was then that Sophie pushed Dylan's heroin buttons.

February 4, 2020
Sophie: *My boy has twenty-five-dollar buns and it's fireeeee. LOL, I'm the worst. I spent so much on an Uber the other day. Hahahaha*
Dylan: *Damn, that sux.*
Sophie: *$110. I was so dopesick and couldn't take the car cuz the damn warrant. Anyway, what are you up to?*
Dylan: *Just hit this kid from Paterson to see if he would meet me somewhere less hot.*

Sophie: Well, I'm going tomorrow if you want to wait, I can pick up for you.

Dylan: That would be great.

Sophie: I just kinda feel bad doing it, I don't wanna be the reason you relapse.

Earlier that day, Dylan had connected with a dealer from his past in Paterson. He ordered blues, (oxycodone). Here's his text with the Paterson dealer:

Dylan: Yoo, it's DC, was good bro?

Dealer: Wassgud, Watchu needed?

Dylan: I was lookin for like at least a brick, maybe 8 tops. But it's been hotboy in Paterson. U got any places that are low key we could meet?

Dealer: Right by my house, how much you pay for ya movies?

Dylan: When I left I was doin 120, 130, u straight to do 8 for 200?

Dealer: Yea, I gotchu my guy. Text me when you in Paterson.

Dylan: Bet. Where am I going so I know what exit.

Dealer: (Provides Dylan an address) and says, hit me when you close.

Dealer: (Contacts Dylan from another phone number) and says his name.

Dylan: Bet.

Dealer: Why u ask where I'm at?

Dylan: So I can head that way. Unless you got wheels.

Dealer: Nah, I don't drive. (Again, he asks Dylan what he needs)

Dylan: Can u do 9 for 200?

Dealer: 9 buns?

Dylan: 9 blues.

Dealer: yeah.

Dylan: Light, and u sure they ain't Fent presses? I don't care either way, just want to be safe.

Dealer: 100 percent bro

Dylan: Cool

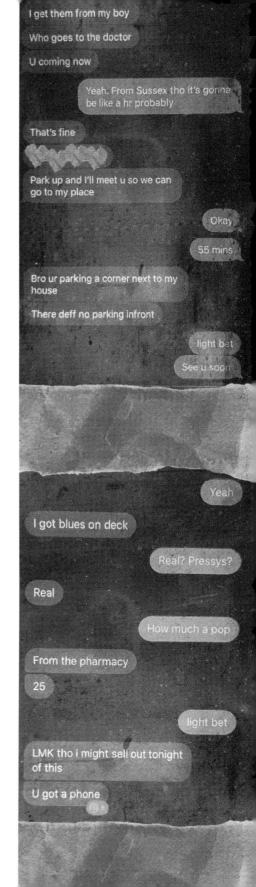

There wasn't enough HOPE joy, or love in his heart. He didn't believe in the possibilities of recovery.

Dealer: *I get them from my boy who goes to the doctor. U coming now?*

Dylan: *Yeah, it's going be like an hour probably.*

Dealer: *That's fine, (he provides Dylan with an address and tells him to park, they'll meet and go to his place).*

When Dylan firmed his heroin order with Sophie, he'd already attained the Xanax and Oxys. This was the point of no return, and from their text exchange, I realized no treatment, medicine, or facility would have saved my son, nor could I. If it hadn't gone down that week, it would have another day, week, month, or year. No matter how street and drug smart he was, Fentanyl would win by killing him.

The irony was he knew it, and coached Sophie about Fentanyl, a hardcore user herself. He knew the vulnerability when exiting recovery centers. There wasn't enough hope, joy, or love in his heart. His inner turmoil and pain were too great. He didn't believe in the possibilities of recovery, and when a substance abuser recovers, what really does that mean? They fight daily, monthly, yearly, and the rest of their days, not to use again. While they watch others grab for a drink, food, other legal, drugs of choice, they must refrain with an inner strength unbearable to most. We expect them to be supersonic where we ourselves, fail. But they did the ugly, and we are still above that. Are we, though?

Returning to Dylan's last day's texting with Sophie, he responds to her fear of him relapsing.

Dylan: *I got blues today anyway. I'm not gonna use a rig.*

Sophie: *Promise? Cuz it def has Fent in it.*

Dylan: *Yeah, for sure, all dope is fent/deluded now. LOL, Sad, I miss the good old days.*

Sophie: *True.*

Dylan: *Be careful with the Fent tho love, please.*

Sophie: *I will, I need to stop doing so much cuz I don't get higher, just throw up. You know what I mean,*

They fear daily, monthly, yearly, and the rest of their days, that they won't use again.

like when you sniff at least it doesn't matter if you do three or six, the high just kinda levels. This dope is like the best I've gotten in a while, so be careful.

Dylan: *Just be safe don't overdue Fent.*

Sophie: *What did you want?*

Dylan: *A brick, I'll give you some.*

Sophie: *Oh damn, I really don't like driving with that much, it makes me nervous. Also, you wanting that much makes me nervous. I'm sure I'll be fine tho I'm just worried if I get pulled over that's a lot to hide. Also, I just assumed you only wanted like a bun so I was going to front you, if you want a brick, I'd have to come get the money first. How about we start with a bun or two? LOL I'll be going down again, trust me.*

On February 5, Sophie delivered the heroin to Dylan. It was midafternoon. They texted during the rest of the day. She asked if he had tried it yet and he told her that he would first come down off the blues. They texted into the evening and the last text she sent was at 10:50 p.m., asking if he had tried it yet or was still coming off the blues. He didn't answer, and another unanswered text from Sophie followed at 10:06 a.m. the following morning.

Most likely, Dylan took his last breath in the early hours of February 6, which as fate would have it, was my father's birthday.

How I decided to handle Sophie was a decision that wouldn't necessarily resonate with another. It was based on part grief, anger, and unchanneled emotions. The shoes from which I walk are soft like a moccasin and include sympathy. The girl wasn't without regard for human life, like a drug dealer who cuts Fentanyl into heroin. Like Dylan, she shared in addiction's dark hell.

Dylan asked for the heroin. After all I had seen, it could have been Dylan who supplied someone with their final dose. How could I blame her for his death? Heroin had

Sophie delivered the **HEROIN** *to Dylan.*

FEB 5, 10:50 PM

Have you tried "it" yet lol or u still coming off the blues ?

FEB 6, 10:06 AM

Morning boo ☠️

FEB 6, 1:30 PM

I hope you didn't misplace your phone again lol

He didn't **ANSWER.**

ambushed this woman's existence. Her mother dispensed her heroin rations.

What do you do when you've done everything humanly possible? You've purged your family, friends, finances, self, exhausted societal institutions, medicines, sciences, therapists, and support groups. I could never imagine being in that mother's place, and how many could never imagine being in mine?

An example of another mother who fluffed her feathers while guarding her toddler's pen. She never predicted she'd go from spoon-feeding peas to spoon-feeding heroin. Life is complicated. We battle our child's demons with a dull sword, swinging until the end — ours, or our child's.

A mother who keeps hope in her heart for that long doesn't deserve criticism or judgment. She needs kindness and love more than anything. People aren't celebrating her child's future, and they're not comforting her during her child's perpetual sickness. She's alone, really alone.

What are the choices but to substitute heroin with Suboxone? Spend days, months, and years replacing the physical throbbing with mental anguish, often dropping the sword while losing the battle.

As much as I wanted to meet her, and have my revenge moment, I was grieving too hard. A uniformed guard would not lead her bowed head and shackled legs to a plexiglass window where she'd be seated, incapable of eye contact. It was 2020, and texting was the way. With Dylan's phone, I called her number and hung up. In a haunting way, I wanted her to see Dylan's name-calling. It worked, later in the day she sent back a text:

March 23, 2020
Sophie: Hey.
Me: Hey.
Sophie: Who's this? I don't have your number saved and
*   have missed a call from today. I'm sorry, I got a*
*   new phone.*

I was

GRIEVING

too hard.

Liberty Grove
Memorial Gardens
Crematory

CREMATORY

Me: Your numbers were transferred to your new phone. You know whose phone this is. I'm Dylan's mother. Will you talk to me? I would appreciate it if you did.

Sophie: I'm sorry, I don't know who you are.

Me: Look at the number you're calling from your contact list and messenger. It's Dylan's phone. I'm his mother on his phone. Do you want me to show u texts?

Sophie: This is a new number.

At this point, I forwarded Sophie a recent text between her and Dylan. I explained that she had blocked me when she saw his Facebook light turn on.

Me: Will you or won't you talk to me? I am not going to bust you. Sophie, just talk to me. I'm guessing you're not going to talk; I wanted some closure. I am not setting you up for a criminal case. You have enough history and problems. It's not worth it as far as I'm concerned. Ok, so I'll be signing off now.

Sophie: Hello? Don't have good service where I am.

Me: Are you home or in rehab?

Sophie: Down the shore, staying with a friend, trying to get into rehab. I'll message you when I get back to her house, I don't have good service right now.

Me: What are you feeling since Dylan's death? Did you use the same bundles as him?

Sophie: Yes, I did use the same. I'm so depressed. I feel horrible.

Me: I know you do, and I should hate and want you dead, but you are the same person as Dylan and hundreds of others.

Sophie: He promised me that he wasn't going to shoot it, and everything was going to be okay. I just can't believe he's gone.

Me: He didn't shoot it. He snorted it.

I am not setting you up for a **CRIMINAL** *case.*

Sophie: I cry every day; he really did only snort it? Dylan was there for me when I lost Sam.

Me: He was as drug smart as they come. He knew people out of rehab always die. I thought at first it was suicide. Then his son found two bundles and oxies in his toy car.

Sophie: He was such a sweet, caring guy. I hate myself. I thought I was helping him out, doing him a favor. He wasn't able to get it, so I went for him. I regret it more than anything. I hate heroin.

Me: I saw all your texts since December. He was supporting your sobriety until January 30. Then I think you kept talking about your bags, and we pressured him to get into a sober house. He got the blues in Paterson, and he caved.

Sophie: He told me he had blues. I didn't want to give him the bags, and he told me if I didn't give them to him, he was going to go get them anyways and more than likely would get arrested.

Me: You're the same as every one of his heroin connections. You're about to die too. Odd that you, too, are still here. I thought the same with Dylan, who survived eight other overdoses, and the 9th took him out. You r ready to check out too. Unless something fucking immense changes you.

Sophie: I'm going to get clean; I have to.

Me: I don't blame you because you are a junkie. In a sense you just delivered for him. The detectives said I could get a case going, but after seeing your text, I saw Dylan in you.

Sophie: I'm just now numbing my emotions because I'm so depressed. Dylan was truly there for me, and I thought I was just helping him out. But now he's dead. I'm so sorry.

Me: Dylan was self-medicating for years. It looks like many of you do the same.

Sophie: I hate myself; I really do. I feel horrible. Did he def do the heroin then? Or did he OD on the

You are

about to

DIE

too,

I only started really talking to Dylan in December.

He was a really good friend that was there for me after 💔

I don't know if you're getting my messages or if I'm not getting yours? Don't have the best service

I saw when your text began. I have read through his history. It brought me a great relief to see how he actually died and how it went down.
We knew a girl in a white car brought him the goods. It was all pieced together. But it wasn't until I got into his phone that I found out who.
I know you're all big time users, addicts etc. you have watched everyone die you know the Patterson, heroin, is deadly. You're too much an addict to stop. Sounds like your childhood was bad and your mother is a mess. What keeps you going and not pulling the trigger?

What keeps you going and not pulling the **TRIGGER?**

blues? Because he said, he was waiting to come off blues first and had fifteen bags.

Me: How can you think supplying someone right out of rehab would help? They will die. Was it because you didn't want to disappoint him? You liked him. Didn't you know the statistics of addicts dying after using directly after rehab?

Sophie: I've literally been thinking about this every day, every day Dylan crosses my mind. I've been using heroin for two years. Never been to rehab only detox twice.

Me: Two bags were used off one bundle and the other bundle untouched. One bag was found at the time of death. He snorted.

Sophie: I only started talking to Dylan in December. He was a really good friend that was there for me after Sam died. I don't know if you're getting my messages or if I'm not getting yours. Don't have the best service.

Me: I saw when your texts began. I have read through it, and it brought me a great deal of relief. I know you're all big-time substance abusers. You have watched everyone die that you know and know the Paterson heroin is deadly. You're too much an addict to stop. It sounds like your childhood was bad and your mother was a mess. What keeps you going and not pulling the trigger?

Sophie: Yes, I've been through a lot but that's life. I am stopping, I have to. My life sucks as it is and it's just making it worse. I just want to go back two years, and I would've never touched heroin. I was taking Roxys for almost nine years. Only started heroin two, two and a half years ago.

Me: Same shit, different day. Addiction is addiction.

Sophie: I just hope that one day my life is happy. I loved Sam, and I miss him too, but he was no good for me. He hurt me, mentally and physically.

Me:	As I told Dylan, happiness comes in moments. How old are you?
Sophie:	32, my life's a joke. My anxiety has gotten so bad and I'm super depressed. Drugs ruined my life.
Me:	You're a baby! I'm 63 and have lost my only baby. Like I used to say to Dylan, pull the fucking trigger or get the fuck up and live the life you were given. He never took his meds properly, so who knows if he would have ever been ok.
Sophie:	No shit drugs ruin life. But WTF? I'm so sorry, you don't understand how bad I feel and you should want me dead. I seriously feel like such a piece of shit. I want to turn back time and change a lot of things and I wish I could.
Me:	What's your plan?
Sophie:	I really miss Dylan; I'm going to go into rehab. But I don't know with all this corona shit.
Me:	You haven't ever been in rehab?
Sophie:	Never, I've done like a seven-day detox and fourteen-day program. But that doesn't really count.
Me:	They're not worth the shit. Just letting you know.
Sophie:	I've gone to detox a few times and relapsed the day I got out. I seriously want to get sober for good.
Me:	Detox, too, is bullshit. What's your plan, is what I'm asking?
Sophie:	I'm just not going to use anymore and try to get sober on my own. I just need to get Subs (suboxone), so I don't get sick. Ugh, I don't know if I can do it myself though. This drug has taken my life. I honestly don't feel like I'm living, it's taken everything from me. My phone may die, and my charger is in friend's car. If it does die, I'll message you when it's back on.
Me:	That's bullshit, Suboxone, and Methadone are all bullshit.

I'm
63 and have
LOST
my only
baby.

SUBOXONE  and METHADONE are all bullshit.

Sophie: *I don't know, what do you think, I was just going to take subs to get off heroin but don't want to be taking them every day.*

Me: *All bullshit! You go cold turkey, no rehab, no sober house. It's all bullshit. I have lived and invested and know many others. It's cold turkey and determination, period! Subs keep you addicted and maintain the system financed.*

Sophie: *I'm going to try and go cold turkey. It's going to be extremely hard.*

Me: *Three days of pain and sickness, you will not die. Just flu symptoms, bite the fucking bullet because the worse challenge is yet to come. How long have you lasted? I've witnessed many opioid withdrawals with Dylan.*

Sophie: *I've gone three days without anything, and yes, it literally felt like I had the flu and I ended up taking a Suboxone. It was horrible, I was puking and going to the bathroom at the same time. I really feel like I should take a half a sub at forty-eight hours and then the other half at four days and then just take nothing more. I don't know if I could do the entire thing cold turkey.*

Me: *Been there, done that dozen times with Dylan. You want out of this fucking madness? Suffer a few days, and it's over. Don't do suboxone or anything. That's what keeps it going. It hurts, is painful, and makes you crazy with anger and physical pain. But if you take the meds, you will never be free of it and just return as you have already, many times before.*

Sophie: *Ok, I'm going to try cold turkey.*

Me: *It's three fucking days. Lay in bed and suffer until it's over. After that is the biggest challenge. My baby my only child is dead, ok? You hear me. You dealt the final blow. You feel that. Get the fuck clean!*

Sophie: I'm so fucking sorry. You know that's the last thing I wanted to happen. Ugh, I hate my fucking self. Phones about to die 1%.

I ended our text string with a heart and prayer hands emoji. Today, I would not use those same words with Sophie. I've learned so much about addiction, cravings, trauma, and the brain. I'm almost three years from the horrific moment of my son's death. I know how much of an illness it becomes, is, was, and how painful a struggle it is to maintain sobriety. Especially when the very cause of substance abuse continues to dwell deeply in the soul.

There are plenty of platforms supporting addiction and families, but not enough supporting the mental illness of addiction, and hazards of addiction recovery centers, prescribed treatments of Suboxone, and psych meds. Society's ignorance of addiction pulverizes substance abusers, and their families. We should never feel the need to hide due to misconceptions of a substance abuser having a choice.

If you take the meds you'll never be **FREE**

In comparison, the parent of a child battling cancer will have a considerable advantage in compassion. Never should a substance abuser's parent feel less worthy when fighting for their child's life. It's an unbearable life for these families, lasting years, possibly until life's end. I hope to be part of the change and continue to be a voice for substance abusers and their families.

The worst part is no one feels sorry for you because they think your child can stop, if only they had the willpower. They don't realize that sometimes life ends in a fatal overdose. How painful for me to realize this after my son's death. I, too, told him just to do it, that he had the power to quit and conquer the voices. I did it with cigarettes years prior. Why couldn't he? I was completely ignorant to the level of pain my son was concealing.

How awful to be lumped into a pit of *society's losers*. The ones you walk by, looking anywhere but into their eyes. If it were another form of death, others would

comfort us. When these people pass on, others look at it as a blessing. It's best that they no longer suffer, take up space on cardboard beds, or share our home while torturing the rest of the family.

I didn't know how to express my son's passing. When confronted with the cause of death, I gestured injecting a needle in my arm. I'm ashamed to say that I thought like the addict early on, not feeling worthy of grief support. At most, it would be insincere. Why even accept someone's condolences when I didn't believe a word anyway.

I didn't want to hear anyone speak
or hear how or how not to be.

I ONLY
WANTED
THING
MY S

14

Living in Silence

During my lifetime, I've buried and cried for many. The grief of losing my son, I do not know how to do. A rolling swell arrives daily. Should I glimpse his photo, risking unstoppable tears slithering down my face? Although eventually, they will stop, that's how it works. I wrote this chapter a week shy of the second anniversary of his death. The cloud no longer shades me, yet his absence remains dreamlike.

Dylan's cellphone is an appendage of sorts, sitting on my desk, still in service. If I cancel service, will I seal the emotional suffocation? It's all I have left besides Pug sandals and a dirty hoodie with "Scumbag" printed on the front.

During my early grief, I declined to join therapy groups or read books on loss. I didn't want to hear anyone speak or suggest how or how not to be. I wanted only one thing: my son on this physical plane.

The pain of grief is love in disguise, with the depths of despair reflecting how deeply we loved. The amount of love you share is how much and how long it will hurt. Which, realistically speaking for all of us, will be forever.

What do I do on Mother's Day? Am I still a mother? Each of us in the same situation will have a different response to that question. I quickly learned how important it was to follow my heart. That's how I handled the first two years of birthdays, anniversaries, and holidays. I didn't force myself to perform another's tango. Our family, friends, and peers tend to overcompensate, thinking we need fixing. It's not their fault that they don't know how

His absence

remains

I could

not bear

SPEAKING

to anyone.

to react. What we choose to do with one person may be entirely off-center for another.

I now know what I didn't realize during early grief. When the fog rolls in, it's best to bunker down, then venture out with a flashlight. That's what worked for me, and someone else may need more support from family, friends, or religious communities.

I could not bear speaking to anyone. My husband's chitchat screeched like fingernails on a chalkboard. Nothing anyone said had meaning nor mattered. My son's death was life's finish line. Even though I expected and felt prepared for it, I was not. I began dueling suicidal thoughts.

Being a mother was an honor, and when my son died, I lost all purpose. The last decade was a continuous rescue and recovery mission. Aside from business duties, I spent my waking hours trying to find his cure.

My Type-A diva image shape-shifted to a lamb, looking down at the cliff's edge. I asked myself, do I jump to the next ledge or into the air and surrender? I've lived long enough and witnessed others crossing over. I would be okay if the lights turned off today.

At times life is just too much effort; why keep going? And for what? There's nothing left to dream. Life does not reward you for being a good scout. Passing days don't get brighter or supply more bandages.

How do I respond when people send me "Happy Birthday" messages or "have a great day?" I wasn't two months into grief when someone asked, "Have you returned to your art studio?" These are innocent questions asked by those who care, love us, and want things to return to normal, as before. Where does a loved one go after the funeral's comfort phase? How often have you heard, "I'm here if you need anything," an empty statement with no meaning.

When I walk by my son's picture, I feel him but cannot look up. How do I describe that feeling? A throat of lumps, preventing gags by swallowing the tears. A contorting jaw competing with quivering lips, squeezing the checks into the eyes then brows. It's an instant replay all day long. When the phone rings, blow your nose, and if asked, it's allergies. No one knows the hours I spend gutted, not even my husband. That's my way, not right or wrong, just my way.

I dedicate this chapter to those who've lost and never had the support or friendship from others who've been where you are. We've had to contain the screams thrashing within our heads. We had to find a way to be larger than life and find patience for others.

The loss of a loved one, especially a child, is life-altering. We proceed down the isle of grief in our way and in our time. It's a painfully individual process.

Shortly after my son's death, having no clue what I was doing, I tried to show up for others. By the third month, it was too high a task. Thanks to Covid, socializing wasn't frequent, and what little I had, remained a gruesome chore. Be the person I had always been — an exhausting character flaw. I felt worthless and that I had failed miserably as a mother. I walked in the woods, fingers of an invisible specter pressed into my back, forcing me to move faster into the thicket. It wasn't a place to hide as much as a place that stripped cognitive senses.

The uncrowning of parenthood began. So much for all those good-parent things: cooking organically, self-expression, music, art lessons, theater, technology, martial arts, and homeschooling.

Dreams of sharing Dylan's future in my early parenthood journals were replaced with darkly worded ramblings that only I understood. And that too was okay. That's how I did grief, with denial bitch-slapping me all the way.

Social attempts

were a

GRUESOME

chore.

15

Lockdown and Grief

Those who suffered loss during Covid lockdown faced the painful task of saying good-bye without the support of family and friends. For many, this would remain the most painful of Covid memories. When we lose a loved one, we need to share our story, be heard, and know that others are experiencing our sorrow. Unable to attend a family funeral is achingly oppressive. Zoom chats do not replace falling into the arms of someone who tightly hugs you while you weep.

Everyone was confined, masked, fighting for their sanity with Lysol strapped to their belt. Poor innocent children lost two years of schooling, sports, and playdates. Who could we share our pain with when the world was on the edge of collapse? Who would die next, how would the bills be paid, and when would supermarkets restock the shelves?

We were in early Covid madness when my son died but were fortunate to hold a small gathering five days before lockdown. When Dylan died, my inability to see life moving forward caused me to turn off social media. Living in isolation allowed me to avoid families' and friends' political and scientific infighting. During the first few months of grief, I remained quiet. I couldn't think, and time didn't matter. There is a peace to that, and the silence was somewhat calming. I grasped what I thought was happening with my grief but soon learned that no belief could carry its painful weight. I wanted to feel okay again.

I awoke to a day like any other, but this one dreadfully redirected the rest of my life. I was not to be one of the lucky ones excused from the agony of losing their child

Fighting for SANITY with Lysol strapped to their belt.

he completed his

earthly agenda,

God calling

his angel

home?

— a scene witnessed of a collapsed screaming parent, grasping their heart. I scared myself. It's impossible, and it's not real. I wanted time to stop the day before.

The tragedy is not selective. It could, and would, also happen to me. Why me? I asked. Well, why not me? It's my only child. Regardless, if I were young enough to create another child, it would never be that child. WHY DID HE HAVE TO GO when I endlessly worked to save him?

Karma, he completed his earthly agenda, God calling his angel home. Or are we no more than an earthworm? Why continue and be when life is often tragic and painful? I no longer had a family without my son, and I wasn't open to being adopted into other families' gatherings. Grief and pain are personal; no one lives in my heart.

The only positive thing about Covid was that I had an excuse to stay isolated. The first holidays and special events following my son's death were unbearable, like being a widow at a wedding. It's a displacement of everything I had dreamed. To expect me to find joy in someone else's holiday traditions did not bring comfort to my broken heart. It was not an option. Not today, not now, maybe someday.

The pain of forcing a smile, faking laughter, suppressing tears, and regrouping thoughts to keep from publicly melting down is what I did while the others carried on with their lives. The energy required to socialize was not worth the effort. It will come in time, without judgment. It wasn't easy, especially with those who felt differently, thinking they could do grief better. The gavel struck the block, and I became handcuffed emotionally. I must find peace and purpose if I'm to continue life. I no longer feared death and lost my will to live.

My grandson was my grief distraction, and he needed me as much as I needed him. If I could look deeper beyond the borders of grief, part of my son still exists in my grandson. Although it hurt a lot when people said, "Well, you still have your grandson," It was a sign that my grief was not validated. I'm supposed to pass it off, get over my son's death, and get on with life. Sweeping the grief

The only positive thing about Covid was that I had an excuse to stay isolated.

under the carpet, confused and unable to exercise gratitude, self-flogging at its best. Furthering my doubt, what of the others who've lost a child without the opportunity of being a grandparent?

I was old enough, tired enough, and beaten down enough to feel I'd done my time. My eyes were blurry, as was my heart. It knew not which way to beat. Its strings pulled from outside and tightened inside. My mind needed to be kept quiet.

I often thought of other parents sharing in this horrific experience of Fentanyl poisoning. I knew they were facing the phone call and visiting the morgue. Having to lift a sheet to identify their baby, say good-bye, and be forced to create funeral plans within hours.

Having to lift a SHEET to identify their baby.

There's an expression for those first days, weeks, and months after losing a loved one — Brain Fog. I can describe it in the following metaphoric language.

Vapored fingers creep underneath the door and grasp my neck as the fog rolls forth. I can't breathe, don't want to, I hurt. I can't think. Where is my brain? Why is everyone saying the wrong thing, melding words in the fog that claws my skin?

People don't know this different person. The door swings open with an invitation to a housewarming. A toothless doorman with burnt hands smiles while waving me on. I don't know why, but he's kind, and I'm not afraid. He's like an old uncle; I feel at home. Everywhere clocks are ticking, but time doesn't change. The bell goes off, signaling my return to the damp, dark, daunting room that became my son's song. He is no longer.

It's what people do with their dead? They keep talking to them, writing letters, and cooking their favorite meals. What can I do? Somehow, I'm to keep memories alive. How can anyone plan to keep alive someone who should not be dead?

Still today, I struggle with not participating in wishing my son a happy birthday or posting his picture in social media on anniversaries. It's not right for me, but I understand it's right for others. I hope to encourage people to accept that we each process our losses differently, and we're to respect the wishes of those we differ from. Many cultures have traditions for death, and still many, are never taught a death etiquette.

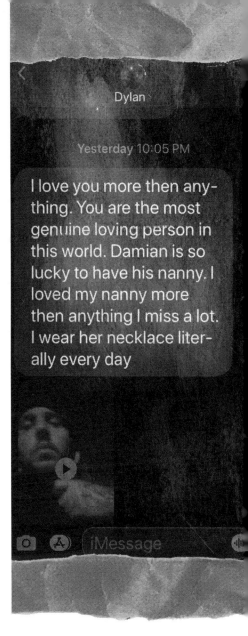

How can anyone plan to keep someone alive who should not be dead?

My grandson's future and all it should have been.

16

Finding Purpose

After the first year of Dylan's passing, I expected my emotions to ease. Instead, they worsened, and I sank deeper into despair. The first year was a shock, and the second made it real. My grandson was a weekly distraction, but when he returned home, I'd emotionally crash. I was trying to sort out my pain from what I projected onto my grandson's future of what should have been.

Sleep became an issue, insomnia, a new friend, the world of podcasts, a consolation to my wakeful hours. One evening I listened to David Kessler, whose work as a grief specialist has spanned more than 40 years. Author of *Finding Meaning, the Sixth Stage of Grief*, David also co-authored with Elizabeth Kubler Ross, *On Grief and Grieving Finding the Meaning of Grief through the Five Stages of Loss*. After listening to David, I ordered his book, and looked at his website, *grief.com*

During Covid lockdown, David created an online Zoom community called Tender Hearts. It was more than perfect timing, and globally connected people who were losing loved ones to Covid or who had lost contact with their social grief groups and therapists. It was a time for most of us to enter the world of Zooming. It's how families, businesses, and schools continued. Although it took a few months to get grounded, life as we knew it would never return.

Tender Hearts was a perfect fit to my windless sail and need of isolation. There were no demands or expectations, and I could participate at my own pace. I cannot praise David and his online community of grief

The world of podcasts, a CONSOLATION to my wakeful hours.

Who will make DECISIONS *when I no longer can?*

members enough for the love and understanding they share. Several days a week, David holds Zoom calls offering a nurturing environment where the grief-stricken can be heard and share their losses. He provides guest speakers, videos, and community sections that include grief of a spouse or child, death by suicide, addiction, etc. He gave so much of himself adding a Grief Educator Certificate Program, sharing decades of expertise. Most of us are "grief illiterate," and through knowledge, we can help make the changes.

Listening to and watching others has taught me a lot about myself. Even though I've lived my life being selfless, my sensitivity to others' losses has heightened. By watching David interact with dozens of grievers, I began my own grief work.

When I was a young mother pushing my toddler on a swing, I never thought about the woman sitting on the bench possibly grieving a recent miscarriage. Or the woman walking by who suffers infertility. And there could have been a senior who lost a grandchild to cancer.

I've learned many lessons through Tender Hearts, especially about *secondary grief.* It's grief that includes what would have been. In my case, I'll never have that mother-and-son dance at his wedding. I'll never see him grow into a man, purchase a home, or become something incredible while giving back to society. To whom do I hand my history and family albums? Who will make decisions when I no longer can? Who will want to hug my sweater when I'm gone? I lost my legacy.

We can't replace our loved ones, but hopefully, we will find a purpose in their lives. And as David says, we will replace our pain with love. It took me a year and a half to hang a photo canvas. I did so for my grandson. I still cannot look at them. Yet I know many others find comfort looking at photos. Our hearts heal in our time, no one else's, and my heart will forever cry.

Grief work has helped me to no longer hold myself accountable for Dylan's death. My only regret is not

We can't replace our loved ones, but hopefully, we will find purpose in their lives.

Know your

RIGHTS

and ask

questions.

having the mental health awareness that I've gained since his passing. Often, Dylan's diagnosis was Bipolar and Major Depressive Disorders. Today, I would have found the source, doctor, addictionologist, biochemistry labs, amino-acid therapy, trauma doctor, instead of allowing psych meds and Suboxone.

I've read that not all doctors, including psychologists, agree on current addiction treatments. Labs continue to experiment with rodents and humans. It's a mix of available or new pharmaceuticals versus our brain's neurochemistry.

I imagine that big pharma is supplying doctors with their research on current medicine. It's up to you to be curious, ask questions, read the lab reports, and speak with several practicing medical professionals from various backgrounds and philosophies.

Not everyone reading this book will have the drive, desire, or patience to sift through medical terminology. That's okay; I share this to let you know it exists, and it's out there if you wish to pursue. If not, know your rights, and ask questions from the medical professionals taking care of your loved one. Always keep records of prescribed medicines, and learn about them on sites such as drugs. com, rxlist.com, YouTube, and other apps that can be download.

I would have loved to have had an opportunity to schedule Dylan a biochemical test to determine what was misfiring in his brain, which if any, neurotransmitter was possibly imbalanced? Perhaps he may have lived with the correct medication, amino acid, and supervision by an expert in addiction, neuroscience, nutrition, and trauma. All this combined with pursuing therapy from a trauma expert, may have saved Dylan.

Depending on your location, possibly start with your primary doctor who may have referrals. Or, carefully, and slowly, search integrative medicine on the internet, being extra diligent when viewing a website. Many are sales agents tied to 800 numbers and are looking for nothing more than an opportunity to pounce onto your heart strings, connecting you to a recovery center. Look at your toolbar's address, page down, and look for disclaimers. Before speaking with anyone, be clear about your knowledge and intentions.

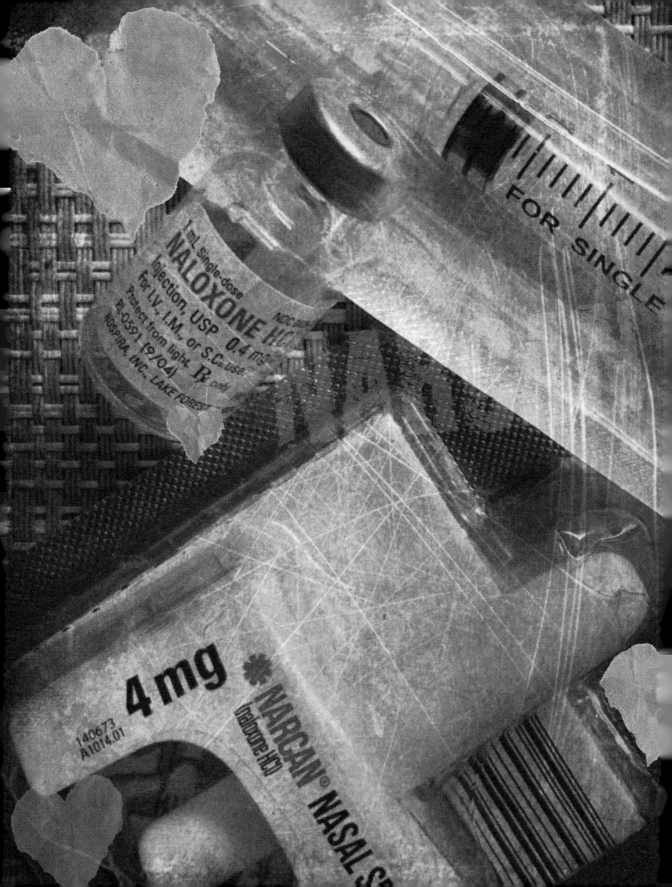

17

Don't Leave Home Without It

If I can end this book with one of the most important messages, it would be to educate you and your family about Narcan. I believe most think it would never happen to my child, but let me say this: yes, it can, and possibly in your home with your child's friend. Especially now, with the Fentanyl crisis. The opioid epidemic's number of deaths is increasing at alarming rates. These deaths account for more than half the yearly stats.

> *"The U.S. government does not track death rates for every drug. However, the National Center for Health Services (NCHS) at the Center for Disease Control Prevention collects information on deaths involving many of the more commonly used drugs available through 2020 at a searchable database, called CDC Wonder."*[1]

In 2020, 70,000 people lost their lives to accidental overdose. In 2021, over 100,000. That's an overdose death every eight to eleven minutes. Almost half of the opioid overdoses involved prescribed opioids. Most happen in the home.[2]

You and your child need to know how to administer NARCAN.

---

[1] Nida.nih.go

[2] Narcan.com

Consider being

a part of the

SOLUTION

to saving

someone's

life.

I believe every household's medicine cabinet should include Narcan. If you have a high-school teen, you and your child need to know how to administer Narcan.

I learned that teens panic when a friend is in the throes of overdosing. Brain damage can occur after four minutes without oxygen; death can occur in seven minutes. They only have seconds to decide to leave them, call the medics, police, or parents. They fear personal repercussions.

Accidental overdose should not be a shunned dinner table chat. Families should include Narcan in the drinking and driving, street drugs, and unprotected sex family talk.

In my youth, I knew a few who lost their lives through drugs and alcohol. Today, due to Fentanyl lacing, just about everything from marijuana to pills, risks overdose and death.

Narcan.com will provide you with a 17-page brochure listing what it is, how to use it, where to get it, etc. It's essential to understand the signs of someone overdosing. Completely understanding how to administer Narcan is vital. Check with your local drug prevention center. Many hold meetings to educate the public and give hands-on demonstrations.

Your insurance carrier may cover Narcan. I purchased mine directly from the pharmacy. Today, many communities distribute free Narcan and training. I carry Narcan in my pocketbook and will forever continue to do so. Please consider being a part of the solution to saving someone's life.

STOP OVERDOSE: The CDC, and most city and state organizations have published a harm reduction strategy with the introduction of Fentanyl Test Strips. These strips can detect Fentanyl in many different drugs. It's a low-cost method that will save hundreds of lives. Spread the word!

They are not trying to get high and happy
as much as they're trying to avoid the pain.

18

Final Thoughts

Unless you've been there yourself, you will never know what it's like to be a substance abuser addicted to drugs or alcohol. You may have an addiction of your own to chocolate, running, smoking, eating, shopping and some other things. The difference with substances is the output of dopamine is greatly increased in comparison. I feel it's important to understand the substance abuser's world, by getting closely inside their head, body, and soul. We can accomplish this by reading books, listening to songs, audible podcasts, watching movies, and live streaming that have to do with substance abuse. Anything you can get your hands on from medical journals to the big screen will bring you that much closer, kinder, and help open your wounded heart.

Most importantly, please hear your child, not the one who comes at you detoxing and vicious, but the one who is fighting not to get *dopesick*. They are not trying to get high and happy as much as they're trying to avoid the pain.

It's difficult, frustrating, and disappointing, but know that the substance abuser doesn't see the way out. Please find the strength from the love you hold in your heart and continue with hope while your child still breathes.

Much love to all of you,
Laura

Resources

There are dozens of choices, these are mere samplings, and some are nostalgic. If I suggest a web search, bc aware that the words 'heroin/addiction' can bring you directly to a *Recovery Center's* website, regardless of the title being otherwise.

MUSIC	Artist(s)	
Needle Damage Done	Neil Young	
Hurt	Nine Inch Nails	Johnny Cash version is great!
Happiness is a Warm Gun	Beatles	
King Heroin	James Brown	
Cold Turkey	John Lennon	
Heroin	Velvet Underground	
Lust for Life	Iggy Pop	
Under the Bridge	Chili Peppers	
Comfortably Numb	Pink Floyd	

MOVIES	
Body Brokers	2021
Beautiful Boy	2018
Candy	2006
Requiem for a Dream	2000
Gridlock'd	1997
Basketball Diaries	1995

STREAMING
Netflix, Hulu, Prime Video   (search addiction)

BOOKS

Brain in Balance	Fredrick Von Stieff, M.D.
Neuroscience of Everyday life	Great Courses

The Addictive Brain	Great Courses
Nutrient Power	William J. Walsh, PhD.
End Your Addiction Now	C. Gant, MD & G. Lewis, PhD.
The Heroin Chronicles	Lydia Lunch, Nathan Larson
The Heroin Diaries	Nikki Six & Ian Gittins
Recovery Freedom from Our Addictions	Russell Brand
Sickening How Big Pharma Broke American Health Care-John Abramson, MD, MSc	
Overdosed America	John Abramson, MD, MSc
The Body Keeps Score	Bessel Van Der Kolk, M.D.
In the Realm of Hungry Ghosts	Dr. Gabor Mate'
The Myth of Normal	Dr. Gabor Mate'

ONLINE

goodreads.com	Books (search heroin/addiction)
studyread.com	Online Education
scholar.google.com	Scholarly Literature
PubMed	34 million citations/biomedical life science & online books
nim.nih.gov	National Library of Medicine, National Institute of Health
nida.nih.gov	National Institute on Drug Abuse, National Institute of Health
samhsa.gov	Substance Abuse and Mental Health Services Administration
drugs.com	Pill identification
rxlist.com	Pill Identification
WebMD.com	Medical Information

Facebook, Instagram, and Tick Tock have dozens of pages dedicated to addiction.

GRIEF BOOKS

On Grief and Grieving	Elisabeth Kubler-Ross, David Kessler
Finding Meaning: The Six Stages of Grief	David Kessler
Healing Through Yoga	Paul Denniston

GRIEF WEBSITES
grief.com
compassionatefriends.org
dougy.org
griefyoga.com

Acknowledgements

Life brings many in and out of our hearts, and only a few will indefinitely remain. It is they who hold your hand through the darkest, brightest, saddest, and happiest of hours. It is they who can step outside of their comfort zone with unyielding love and support. I call them lifers, and without them, I would lose sight of my soul.

At first, it felt romantic to share that I was writing a book, and against all odds, I finished. Each time I crashed and burned, I reviewed the book's financial commitment I had made in 2021, an aching catalyst that kept me going. But more importantly, more than money could ever value, I promised my son, Dylan, I would get the book written. We had a deal to do this together, and WE did! His phone texts are his voice. His argumentative spirit, documentation, and never stepping down, is his voice. His suffering, that I still feel in my heart, is his voice. I hope that I did him justice, and his death will never be in vain.

Every now and then life deals us a blackjack, mine is my amazing daughter from another mother, friend, and editing guru. She rescued me during creative, emotional chaos, while teaching me how to frame integrity, guiding the book back to its original intention, and never scarring my ego. Her corrections, and advice, were academic, with a bowl of cookie dough to lick in the end.

I never dreamed to ask my bestie, Angela, to share her graphic mastery. She saw my vision, book's potential, and through her magic, offered to visually bring Dylan's voice to each chapter. The gift of time, and selflessness, shall be rewarded the rest of my years with NYC, Artichoke Pizza & Rosa Mexicana, Margaritas.

My dear friend, Davina, has elongated Buddha ears and holds two heart-shaped pom poms. While many disappeared during my early grief, Davina grasped the helm in the roughest of seas.

When I believed that laughter would never be possible, my Icelandic friend, Eyjolfur, sent dark-witted memes. Something I'd forever miss from Dylan. A few weeks following Dylan's death, Eyjolfur forwarded a Winston Churchill quote, "If you're going through hell, keep going." I pocketed the wisdom.

Thank you to my heartfelt lifers, Elaine, who brought food for the heart and soul, and herself, is grieving the loss of her beautiful daughter, Laurel. Jeff & Karen, who pulled me out of my Covid cave by sharing happier memories in handwritten cards. Cyndi, for her intuitive hearts when there were no words. During early grief, my Canadian clan of very special women bestowed constant, unimaginable love and support. Sending forever heartfelt hugs to Diane, Marina, Fay, and Jackie. Although no longer here, Kim, thank you for the push. You are always in my heart. Samantha, it's no coincidence that our reconnection was divine timing. Your education, career history, and immense compassion have added so much integrity and justice to the book. I'm forever grateful. My dearest grandson, Damian, you keep my heart pumping, and without you, I'm not sure I'd have had the strength. Thank you, Jackie, for loving Dylan through thick and thin and for giving me the most precious gift, a grandson. Lastly, to my husband, Skip, for always supporting my dreams, helping me create the space required to nurture myself, art, and this book. Our life has been greatly challenged but we continue to share the shovel. It's not what life becomes, but what's always been.

There are many I love, who have continued to extend softness to my grieving heart, they know who they are. I don't easily share my life these days, and when I do, it's with those who count. Those who understand what it is to love, be loved, and give love. We are the fortunate ones, for there is nothing else on earth that matters. If you can find a way to love the spider dangling from your ceiling, you've reached the summit.

About the Authors

Laura is a native New Yorker, born and raised in the Bronx. In her early teens, her family moved to New Jersey, where she has remained except for a few years spent in breathtaking northern Arizona. When her son and co-author, Dylan, passed away in 2020, Laura's dedication shifted from ceramics instruction to grief education. She earned a Grief Educator Certificate from renowned grief specialist, and author, David Kessler, and she continues to study trauma and grief. Laura also advocates against stigmas tied to substance abusers and their families. She cultivates an Instagram and Facebook page, *hearts_loss_and_grief*, to support the bereaved, share appropriate grief language, and shed stigmas of substance abuse. When Laura, who resides in rural NJ, is not raising Monarch butterflies, gardening, and saving injured wildlife, she's twirling with her bestie on the streets of Manhattan.

Dylan lost his battle with addiction four days after his 26th birthday. He loved his friends, gaming, dark-witted jokes, and staying up all night making music and memes for social media. He was a loving father to his son Damian, his life force inspiration, and his reason to fight as hard as he did during his last year of life. Without his contributions to this book, it would not have been written.

Made in the USA
Columbia, SC
02 December 2023

27616454R00111